1974

This bo...

The Self Beyond

TOWARD LIFE'S MEANING

Benjamin S. Llamzon

LOYOLA UNIVERSITY PRESS
Chicago 60657

LIBRARY OF CONGRESS
CATALOGING IN PUBLICATION DATA

Llamzon, Benjamin S., 1928
    The self beyond.

    Bibliography: p.
    1. Life.   2. Self (Philosophy).   I. Title.
BD431.L48   126   72-10323
ISBN 0-8294-0217-9

I wished to live deliberately, to front only the essential facts of life, and see if I could not learn what it had to teach, and not, when I came to die, discover that I had not lived. I wanted to live deep and suck out all the marrow of life.

H. D. THOREAU

To my wife and sons
Shirley, Teddy, and Vincent.
In unlimited wholing of our lives together.

CONTENTS

PREFACE

It is almost fifty years since J. C. Smuts, author of *Holism and Evolution* and that rare combination of soldier-statesman-philosopher and diplomat, wrote in the foreword to Monsignor Kolbe's "book," *A Catholic View of Holism*:

> It was a great matter of gratification to me that, on the appearance of *Holism*, Msgr. Kolbe at once acknowledged himself a Holist. I hailed him as a convert. There I was wrong. And he has written this interesting Essay to prove that Holism is older than my book, that it is at least as old as Christianity, and that St. Paul was the greatest holist of them all. So be it. I waive all claim to priority before such august competition.[1]

Since all the pages of this book revolve around the part-whole theme as the meaning of life, and since this theme is reflected in varying degrees of explicitness in countless works past and present, "waiving all claim to priority" is for me both easy and necessary. Why then this book?

I may perhaps be allowed to mention two reasons. First, I believe the way a man wrestles with a problem necessarily tints the conclusion he reaches from his own particular vantage point. The person is a method in himself, necessarily contained in his own meaning. Thus an answer of identical words may bear different contents, depending on the vantage point from which the answer issues forth. What I am saying is really nothing more than the distinction, common today among linguistic analysts, between "sentence" and "statement." So while the word "whole" that I employ is the selfsame one that is used in other versions, my scope carries its own differentiating content, I hope, because it is at once narrower and wider than the earlier versions of holism. I confine my attention here exclusively to the puzzle of human life, not the whole of reality. And though I consider the problems of God and immortality matter in themselves for endless books, I treat them here, no matter how briefly, as unavoidably related to the meaning-of-life question.

Secondly, I may point out the peculiar use of the English word "whole" in this book. Previous books which touch on the meaning of life as a matter of "building wholes" do not use the word in its verb form. The reason is plain. One searches English dictionaries, large and small, in vain for any clue that the word may once have been a verb. Yet, it *was* a verb at one time, as noted in the *Oxford English Dictionary*, vol. XII, p. 92:

> *Whole*, v. obs., also, hoole, hold. 1. trans. to make whole, heal, cure. 2. intr. to become whole, to recover from sickness, to heal, as a wound; 3. to make into a whole, to assemble, to unite as "The captaine wholed a multitude of people gathered of divers Nations . . . and beginneth a commonwealth after this manner."

The illustrative sentence in the text above may itself be of some relevance to our times, when the question of life's meaning arises out of all the agonies of a fragmented society. While no one hopes to penetrate the mystery of human living completely, it is my hope nevertheless that insights and ideas forged in classroom reflections and by the firesides of friendly warmth may fruitfully find their way to wider "wholes." Let me explain.

I think there is a very real sense in which every philosophy teacher is a method in himself. Whatever conclusions he reaches, whatever questions he poses, he does so only by virtue of the sifting process fashioned by his own personality, interest, and professional competence. This book was literally born in my classrooms and in those spheres of personal space that Marcel has pointed out as the places where one "receives" the other into his being whenever the enfleshment of the spirit comes into being. No one, not even a professional philosopher, reads everything, talks to everybody, probes every experience and situation with the same rigor and intensity. Personal selection **cuts** its individual way clear through all the masses of possible material, selecting, pursuing, savoring, brushing aside, digesting, and in general nurturing the growth of an insight. All these processes are suffused with individuality. Why? Because the originating force as well as the touchstone in philosophical composition is ultimately the *self*. One chooses nothing in philosophy that does not deepen self-knowledge. I do not think this can be disputed, unless one is prepared to impugn Socrates' characterization of philosophy as "self-knowledge." Thus, though the theme of part-whole I pursue in this book is not novel, there is, I hope, a tint of novelty in the method of its unfolding.

The tang of living comes, to a great extent, in baring one's self to others. This is done in countless ways, one of which is publication. Certainly there is an intimate relation between publishing and "teaching philosophy," just as there is in engaging in a philosophical search for truth with trusted friends. Elsewhere in this book I take a position on the problem of the self. Suffice it to say here that to the extent there is a problem of "teaching philosophy," that problem eventually resolves itself into a problem of the self. Either the teacher or the student or both are failing somewhere in that most vital interactive event, namely, the search for *self*. For from the pre-Socratics to Aristotle to Blondel to the neo-Freudians and Christian theologians of today, we find a consensus that the life of self-searching is the highest and richest form of life available to human experience. Thus a philosophical encounter is always a thrilling event, since it is a movement toward life at its finest. Conversely, whenever a philosophy class or conversation goes dead, it does so because the faces of those philosophizing have somehow turned away from each other, thereby putting an end to the search. What one does then is a question to be taken up later in this book.

I think it is fair to say that the role of pedagogical cleverness in teaching philosophy consists in the use of techniques and imaginative devices for making the student search himself. It is not always as easy to do this with the comparatively young as it is with those whose mass of unsorted living generates a longing for philosophical scrutiny. Anyone who has taught philosophy at separate periods during weekend classes, night classes, and day classes has experienced this difference. And that is why philosophical conversation, too, among friends whose faces are turned trustingly toward each other, is one of the purest joys of life, as C. S. Lewis once noted. In the end, self-examination, like Freudian therapy, needs an other with whom we verbalize our findings as we move along. The meeting of two actualities (the only "place" for potentiality)[2] is what philosophical learning and teaching is all about—a point I hope to develop in another work. For now let me just say that on the matters about which I philosophize in this book I have had many joyful encounters with students and friends. I think it is time now to risk a wider encounter. For unlike Freud I do not believe that the human self is archaeologically all of a piece in all of us. Man is a point of free, not deterministic, consciousness. The variety of individual experiences and the openness of man's freedom constitute a far more rewarding vantage point for philosophical seeking than a view of the self as an archaeological relic with the same predictable story lurking behind individual hieroglyphics.

Finally, a specific word on my procedure. Philosophical methods always overlap one another, and if one must declare a position I suppose mine would be that of reflective realism on actual life situations. I cluster possible answers from various thinkers around a question I raise. No comprehensive treatment of those thinkers is attempted. Instead, I make recurrent use of them, each time from a different standpoint as the theme of the book develops. I think this procedure ties itself in realistically with the meaning-of-life question as one lives it. For while a certain amount of order and organizing of the lived world is indispensable to philosophizing, anyone who has taught philosophy along too systematic or too rigorous lines will appreciate the reactive distrust students come to have about the continuity between such modes of thought and human living.

The reader should be especially watchful in Chapter II, easily the most difficult section of the book even after what seemed an endless sorting out of material. I try to unite there many vectors of thought which separately by themselves could issue into whole books. Perhaps I should have divided and subdivided relentlessly with decimal numbering as Lonerganians are wont to do, but then again it may be just that much nearer the *lebenswelt* and the meaning-of-life question not to have done so.

My footnotes are numbered consecutively within each chapter, which should make them somewhat easier to use and, I hope, even enjoy occasionally. Henry Thoreau's (1817-1862) words, which I have bannered at the beginning of this book, and his exquisite distinction between professors of philosophy and true philosophers—which just may have something to say to our times, when philosophy courses tend to receive less esteem than they deserve—are what I would like this book judged by, ultimately. This is how he puts the distinction:

> There are nowadays professors of philosophy, but not philosophers. To be a philosopher is not merely to have subtle thoughts, nor even to found a school, but so to love wisdom as to live according to its dictates, a life of simplicity, independence, magnanimity and trust.[3]

It remains for me to render tribute to all those who have helped me write this book. No special acumen is needed to see that every person whose path in life crossed mine, no matter how briefly, has probably helped me in my philosophizing on the meaning of life. How then can I possibly thank them all by name? The "tears of things" blur a number of those seemingly irretrievable relationships, but I am grateful nevertheless.

No general thanks will do, however, to friends who actively helped me in this project. My special tribute therefore goes to the following colleagues in our philosophy department at Loyola University of Chicago.

Dr. Mary Schaldenbrand, who for three years, on many a joyful occasion, encouraged and supported me in this work, and who read the entire manuscript at the end.

Father David Hassel, S.J., by now not just a philosophical colleague but a brother. I learned many insights from him, even though I did not always follow his painstaking corrections throughout the manuscript. *Amicus certus in re incerta cernitur.*

Father Lothar Nurnberger, S.J., who read parts of my script, and whose vast erudition and friendship I consider myself privileged to enjoy.

Dr. Thomas Wren, for expert editing of large portions of the manuscript.

Dr. Francis J. Catania, philosophy department chairman, for pointing my courses and schedule toward this project.

Father F. Torrens Hecht, S.J., my former chairman, for his kind encouragement and confidence in my endeavors.

At Loyola, I also wish to thank R. P. Mariella and M. E. Creighton, S.J., dean and associate dean of the Graduate School respectively, and the research committee for grants-in-aid; Mr. R. Fry, Sister R. Stalzer, our reference librarians at Cudahy Library, and Mrs. G. Sieben of St. Mary of the Lake Library; Mrs. H. Bruce and Sharon Sullivan of the Grants Office. Would there were a way, too, of communicating my gratitude to every graduate and undergraduate student who struggled through these questions patiently with me in class and after class! My problem is not that I do not remember them; I remember them only too well, so that to list them all here would undoubtedly provoke editorial wrath—a most undesirable situation.

I also happily acknowledge my debt to: Sister Mary Regina of St. Athanasius in Evanston; Dr. Vincent Punzo of St. Louis University; Dr. Gerald Kreyche of De Paul University; Sister Louise French of Mundelein College. Philosophical dialogues with them were always stimulating. In that light, I should certainly mention Fathers F. Copleston, J. de Finance, and J. Lotz, all of the Society of Jesus, whose writings, lectures, and conversations, enjoyed during a teaching stint in Rome, continue to influence me.

As this manuscript goes from his desk to press, my indebtedness to Father Daniel L. Flaherty, S.J., former executive editor of *America* and now of Loyola University Press, is immeasurable. Everything of merit in this book is the beneficiary of his exacting professionalism, editorial skill, and—not least of all—natural good cheer.

My deepest gratitude is reserved for Shirley, my wife of unbreakable faith in good times and bad, professional or otherwise. She was the main sharer of my idea of "wholing," from the beginning all the way to this happy moment. My thanks also go to my sister, Vicenta, who helped me prepare the index for this material.

Need I add that none of these persons I have mentioned is to be linked in any way whatsoever with defects this work may have? All shortcomings here are to be attributed to my own self exclusively. In this there is no *beyond*.

B.S.L.

Loyola University, Chicago

BEYOND THE BOULDER
OF SISYPHUS

In his novel *Mother Night*, in a chapter called "Ah, Sweet Mystery of Life," Kurt Vonnegut portrays the desperate woman Resi beseeching her lover thus:

> "Then tell me what to live for—anything at all. It doesn't have to be love. Anything at all!" She gestured at objects around the shabby room, dramatizing exquisitely my own sense of the world's being a junk shop. "I'll live for that chair, that picture, that furnace pipe, that couch, that crack in the wall! Tell me to live for it, and I will!" she cried. "Just tell me what it should be!"[1]

Resi's outburst is as graphic a statement as any meaning-of-life question that bedevils everyone at one time or another. What is human living all about?

The question dawns on individuals in various ways. Sometimes it arises out of a dramatic crisis, as Vonnegut has pictured it. Quite often, however, it arises simply from a feeling of futility, of going routinely from event to event until one wakes up to the full impact of the French proverb: *Tout c'a change, tout c'est la même chose* ("The more things change, the more they remain the same"). Routine eats its way even into the most varied and zestful life. And we have ample illustration in the art and literature of the world to support Freud's belief that, on balance, human life is more a matter of endurance than enjoyment.[2] And the German philosopher Immanuel Kant (1724-1804) put it bluntly:

> The value of life for us, if it is estimated by that which we enjoy (i.e. happiness) is easy to decide. It sinks below zero. For who would be willing to enter life anew under the same conditions?[3]

Albert Camus (1913-1960), a French existentialist, took "life is absurd" as the theme of his book *The Myth of Sisyphus*. In Greek mythology, Sisyphus was a giant condemned by the gods to roll a tremendous boulder up a mountain, only to have it roll down again to the nether regions, whereupon Sisyphus must needs go down and roll the rock uphill again for all eternity. Is not the analogy to daily living clear? Men in their daily tasks, commuting from home to work and back, usually nine to five, nine to five, back and forth—and for what? Just to continue living? Is it worth paying all that overbalance of pain for life's disproportionately few joys? Does it seem intelligent to keep wanting to pay that overbalance, all the time admitting it *is* an overbalance—a price too high? For Camus at least the answer is summed up in his sentence that there is only one serious philosophical problem a man must at some time settle in his mind: "Why not suicide?" Unless of course, after the fashion of one character in Vonnegut's *Cat's Cradle*, one simply holds that "we doodely do, what we muddily must, until we bodily bust," and so much the worse for philosophy.

One does, surely, meet people who plod on daily in the same unvarying schedule and seem quite content. They do not seek novelties and excitements. Or so they say. Perhaps a good example was the mother of philosopher George Santayana during her years in Boston. Mrs. Santayana, Spanish by birth, had adventurously sailed the seas to England, the United States, and even the far-flung islands of the Philippines back in the days when that country was still Spanish domain. One day she married an American on a British man-of-war in the middle of

Manila Bay to skirt legal prohibitions. When this husband died, however, she married a Spaniard and decided to live in Boston. There she kept away from the get-togethers of neighboring housewives and the busywork of meetings and copying minutes her neighbors thrived on. When they came at last to cluck their resentment and to ask what in the world she ever did with her time, the self-reliant Mrs. Santayana dismissed them with the unsmiling reply, "I try to keep warm in winter, and cool in summer." Her philosopher son exclaims admiringly that not even Diogenes could improve on that statement— which only redoubles one's wonder at the original statement.[4]

We have to keep in mind, of course, that this is narrated by an admiring son, and great philosophers are not any less immune to the sway of feeling when penning even their loftiest thoughts. Moreover, George Santayana (1863-1952) wrote this when he himself was quite literally penning his thoughts on the "venom of existence" and the beauty of "essences" that one contemplates in solitude "for the splendor of it, like the splendor of the sea and the stars." Today one can still see in Rome the place where Santayana lived as a recluse for a great part of his life. His room had a balcony that opened out to a view of the Baths of Caracalla, half-hidden in their ancient ruins among the uncannily beautiful umbrella pines, while underneath the notorious traffic congestion of Rome snarled away thoroughly screened from the great philosopher's view. It seems obvious that the memory of his parent's inner strength confirmed him in his own life-style. And finally, one notes that the Santayanas had enough material income, "genteel poverty" though they called it.[5]

This last observation points up the philosophical character of the meaning-of-life question. One can, of course, avoid it by refusing to think about it. On the other hand, one cannot very well stop his routine to reflect on the question if to stop means starvation. Even a philosopher jumps away from his desk to cope with the situation when he perceives a flood in his basement spreading toward him. "Animal faith" takes over and one strains as though life is worth all one's efforts! Only after the "coincident point between *having* and *being*," as we shall call it in the next chapter, is either secured or desperately lost does the meaning-of-life question reappear hauntingly. In other words, can Camus' philosophical question, "Why not suicide?" occur to any but those who, paradoxically, have enough material comfort (certainly a relative point, as we shall see) to afford the leisure of reflection, or to those who have desperately lost it? *Why?*

There are people one meets who are quick to assert that the meaning-of-life question bothers only the selfish and self-centered people who, in absolutizing themselves, very soon found that self-idolatry is invariably unrewarding. The implication here is that the true meaning of life is simply "being for others," living for my wife and children, for my friends, etc. If the problem were solved that simply, though, it would not be the perpetual torment it is. For as one unselfish individual jokingly mused, "I am betrayed by friends only about seven times a day!" Betrayals aside, however, a little thought will show that the meaning of life is as much a question for altruistic as for unaltruistic individuals. The question is: what are those others for that I should be for them? For others? And those others for others again, ad infinitum? Is this not in effect to make a religion of humanity?

On the unbelievableness of this position William James (1842-1910) has written:

> Many of us, indeed, would openly laugh at the very idea of the strenuous mood being awakened in us by those claims of remote prosperity which constitute the last appeal of the religion of humanity. We do not love these men of the future keenly enough; and we love them perhaps the less the more we hear of their evolutionized perfection, their high average longevity and education, their freedom from war and crime, their relative immunity from pain and disease, and all their other negative superiorities. This is all too finite, we say; we see too well the vacuum beyond. It lacks the note of infinitude

and mystery, and may all be dealt with in the don't care mood. No need of agonizing ourselves or making others agonize for these creatures just at present.[6]

One can perhaps object that being for others *right now*, especially others I love, has in actual experience nothing to do with all those distant others derided in James' passage. There is something awry, it will be said, in holding that what is undesirable in the ultimacy is also undesirable in the immediacy. This is substituting one's abstractions for the concrete situation —what A. N. Whitehead (1861-1947) called "The Fallacy of Misplaced Concreteness."[7] Parents do give themselves to their children in generous and happy love without bothering their heads in the least about all those men of the future who are conjured up for our imagination only by overly serious philosophers. One can say in reply, too, that if the question is merely rhetorical, really intended to block all further philosophical inquiry, then it would be silly to waste time in replying.

But if the position is put forth as a philosophical one, then it must be asked whether it is not true that love for those immediately around us bears along with it a longing, even in the staunchest stoic, that love's fruits endure. It is one thing to suppress this longing and to adopt a stoic, "grin and bear it" attitude, no matter how successfully. It is another matter to philosophize on that very human longing that the efforts of one's life somehow continue to be. This is why it seems impossible to cut off so neatly one's immediate giving of self to others from the question of what those others and indeed all men are for. And it may be why God is sometimes injected into the picture in a way that may seem abrupt to many. As Charles Hartshorne (1897–), a contemporary American philosopher, has written:

> Humanity is an adequate object of unstinted devotion only if there is in man something which stretches beyond and above men: some trait of the universe which calls for our effortless attachment and services: a trait which is permanently there and for all men. One cannot really

have faith in human life while supposing that the cosmic background is unpurposive and insensible. For we face the prospect of ultimate extinction, not only of the individual but of the race, and thereby see that for the final, really long-run perspective, life (without immortality or God) can accomplish nothing, and good deeds as much as bad will eventually produce the same nullity. It is useless to say the better is better as long as you are alive. For when you and the rest are nothing, there is then no better and no worse for your sojourn, if the universe also forgets. To suppose otherwise is merely an illicit fancy that there is after all a cosmic memory, which is a partial reintroduction of a God into the world.[8]

That makes the point quite well. And yet it really is no answer to the meaning-of-life question to say the world or God will remember and save our accomplishments. First of all, we really do not know what "cosmic memory" could possibly be in the ultimate state, and therefore we could not make it the meaning of our lives. Secondly, even if we take God as the meaning of life, we would still have to say that this meaning must be continuous and not separate from the events and course of our life. God as the meaning of life for me must in some way be discernible to me in this life itself. (Bonhoeffer, as we shall see shortly, makes this point quite emphatically.) To deny this would really come down to holding that there is no meaning of life *here*, but only *hereafter*, beyond death. Suddenly, when human life is over, it takes on meaning—this is nonsense. Even if we refine the phrase "human life" as used above and admit one continuous human life in the human soul here and hereafter, it still would make no sense to relegate the meaning of life discontinuously to the hereafter. We insist: if meaningfulness is said of one continuous life, then meaningfulness itself must be continuous and thus somehow present right "here." Hence God should not be abruptly imported into the discussion. The search for meaning in life must be conducted in its own terms.

The terms are that though on the one hand the world and life seem to be meaningless, there are nevertheless moments when we seem able to discern patterns, designs in the events of our lives which stir up hope that greater unfoldings will follow. Writers on Camus' statement do not always point it out, but Camus himself viewed the absurdity of life in a much more complex way. What is clear is that his concept of life's absurdity goes together with his rejection of the hereafter as the meaning of life:

> I don't know whether this world has a meaning that transcends it. But I know that I do not know that meaning and that it is impossible for me just now to know it. What can a meaning outside my condition mean to me? I can understand only in human terms. What I touch, what resists me—that is what I understand. And these two certainties—my appetite for the absolute and for unity and the impossibility of reducing this world to a rational and reasonable principle —I also know that I cannot reconcile them.[9]

More precisely, Camus points out that it is not the world itself that is absurd, but the human longing for meaning vis-à-vis a world that resists, a world that refuses, so to speak, to yield up a meaning.

> I said the world is absurd, but I was too hasty. This world in itself is not reasonable, that is all that can be said. But what is absurd is the confrontation of this irrational and the wild longing for clarity whose call echoes in the human heart. The absurd depends as much on man as on the world.[10]

Vonnegut seems to make the same point in his novel *Cat's Cradle*, when he pictures a character who whispers "busy, busy, busy" whenever life's details become overwhelming. Or again in the rhythmic singing of the calypso-psalm:

> Tiger got to hunt,   Tiger got to sleep
> Bird got to fly,   Bird got to land
> Man got to sit and wonder   Man got to tell himself
> "Why, why, why?"   He understand.[11]

Or as Vonnegut's character Lieutenant O'Hare says in *Mother Night*, after he has captured the double-agent Campbell:

> Just when you think there isn't any point to life, then all of a sudden you realize you are being aimed straight at something.[12]

And yet, for Vonnegut, life's meaning comes down to one word, one exclamation: "This is it: Nothing!"[13] That's putting it bluntly, but is it any different from Camus' "revolt" against the absurd, a revolt expressed through sheer quantitative living?

> What counts is not the best living, but the most living. To two men living the same number of years, the world always provides the same sum of experiences. It is up to us to be conscious of them. Being aware of one's life, one's revolt, one's freedom, and to the maximum, is living, and to the maximum.[14]

With poetic beauty, the American philosopher John Dewey (1859-1952) writes on the essentially mixed condition of things in nature and man. Everything is a profound mixture of what is both stable and precarious:

> We live in a world which is an impressive and irresistible mixture of order and uncertain possibilities, processes going onto consequences as yet indeterminate. They are mixed not mechanically, but vitally like the wheat and tares of the parable. We may recognize them separately, but we cannot divide them, for unlike wheat and tares they grow from the same root.[15]

The implication of this living mixture of the regular and the unpredictable may be gathered from the fact that:

> Germanic tribes had over a thousand distinct sayings, proverbs, and apothegms concerning luck. The world is a scene of risk. It is darkest just before dawn; pride goes before a fall; the moment of greatest prosperity is the moment most charged with ill-omen, most opportune for the evil eye. Plague, famine, failure of crops, disease, death, defeat in battle, are always just around the corner, and so are abundance, strength, victory, festival and song.[16]

What then are we to make of this confusing mixture in reality as regards our lives? Dewey continues:

> This fact is nothing at which to repine and nothing to gloat over. It is something to be noted and used. If it is discomfiting when applied to good things, to our friends, possessions, and precious selves, it is consoling to know that no evil endures forever; that the longest lane turns sometime, and that the memory of nearest and dearest grows

dim in time. The important thing is measure, relation, ratio, knowledge of the comparative tempos of change.[17]

It is interesting to see how even thinkers who profoundly believe in God seek the meaning of life right here with the same passion and agony as thinkers who accept no reality beyond this universe. Thus we recall how John Henry Newman (1801-1890) in his famous sermon *Second Spring* pointed up an insight about human living very similar to the one Dewey talks about in the passage just quoted. The regular pattern of the universe around us, ever breaking through in constant changes, "teaches us," says Newman, "in our height of hope ever to be sober, and in our depths of desolation never to despair."

Dietrich Bonhoeffer (1906-1945), the Protestant martyr to Nazi brutality, is even more insistent that belief in God and the ultimate things cannot substitute for a genuine effort to make sense out of life. Too often, he says, the believer solves all of life's puzzlements simplistically under the rubric of "God's will," which is really just a reiteration of the fact of man's puzzlement and no attempt at an answer at all. "To put it plainly," he says, "for a man in his wife's arms to be hankering after the other world is, in mild terms, a piece of bad taste, and not God's will. We ought to find and love God in what he actually gives us."[18]

Bonhoeffer stresses the point we have been trying to make of finding a meaning of life continuous with what is beyond life, yet never at any moment letting that *beyond*, all by itself, stand as an answer:

> . . . God is no stop-gap; he must be recognized at the centre of life, not when we are at the end of our resources; it is His will to be recognized in life, and not only when death comes.[19]

And again, we find him grappling even with the idea of "fate," which anyone who has experienced the pain of trying to make sense out of life has at one time or another looked to for relief. But unlike Nietzsche's *amor fati*, Bonhoeffer's "fate" is open to

God's transcendence. This is the way he attempts to explain it and resolve the problem:

> We must confront fate—to me the neuter gender of the word "fate" (*Schicksal*) is significant—as resolutely as we submit to it at the right time. One can speak of "guidance" only on the other side of the two-fold process, with God meeting us no longer as Thou, but also "disguised" in the "It"; so, in the last resort, my question is how are we to find the "Thou" in this "It" (i.e. fate) or in other words, how does fate become guidance?[20]

We need not extend this portrayal of the meaning-of-life question any further. It is clear that we cannot hope to break through it in any way unless we first clarify for ourselves what we take man to be. It is only because man is first of all a puzzle to himself that what he is *for* appears as an overwhelming question. And he is a puzzle to himself largely because of a certain plurality in him which makes him wonder who he really is. Before we can solve more ultimate questions, therefore, we must try to determine this: What or who is a man's real self?

BEYOND PERFORMANCE
TO THE SELF

It is safe to say that no problem in philosophy is as complex as the problem of the human self, and that philosophical works on man far outnumber those in other branches of philosophy. No being in our experience is at once so complex and perplexing, and yet so near and challenging, as our own human selves. We are with ourselves always. Always we drive ourselves onward in this business of understanding ourselves, under pain of "sickness unto death." In this chapter then, we shall: (1) approach the problem of the self in as direct a way as possible; otherwise, in a matter like this, one quickly loses the forest for the trees; (2) point up the necessary connection between the problem of self and the realm of ethics; (3) propose an answer; (4) explain and develop that answer further in the light of some competing answers as well as in the light of some objections that might be raised against it.

Needless to say, we can move only in general lines here and not try to identify every position philosophers have adopted on this perplexing question of self. Still, we shall single out some positions for lengthier treatment. It is my hope that this approach, which follows the spontaneous contours of the problem itself, will be preferable to the usual philosophical method of presentation of problem, list of philosophical opinions, elimination, advocacy, etc.

1 THE PROBLEM OF SELF

Anyone of adult age must have asked himself at some time or other: Who am I, anyway? Who is the real I, the *self* in me?[1] The question comes out of a realization that a puzzling plurality is present in man. If a human being were just one simple unity, the question—which in itself presupposes one who asks and one who is asked simultaneously—could not arise. Whatever other complexities there are in man, and there are many, they all seem peripheral to this cleft at the center of his being, his consciousness. Man's consciousness unifies his being even as it radically divides it. This consciousness contains within itself simultaneously the plurality of questioner and questioned.

Furthermore, it is this same human consciousness that offers several possible answers to the question it raises. Still further, it is this same consciousness that judges which of the "candidates" for the title of *self* really is "the man himself." Wherever the elusive self may finally be tracked down, whether in the questioned or questioner side of man, we seem unable to go beyond consciousness itself for judgment. It is this self-sufficient structure of intellectual reflection that underlies the problem of self, and which the contemporary novelist Kurt Vonnegut noted intriguingly when he wrote: "We are what we pretend to be; so we must be careful what we pretend to be."

Pretensions are actions, are they not? Our first impulse then is to equate actions with the man himself. Let us think on it. Is a man's real self his actions (whether individual or collective)? That is to say, the summation of all his actions up to the present? There are good reasons for thinking so. Ancient Greek philosophers, for instance, argued that a completely inert being would not be even knowable. For to be known is to enter into a relationship of sorts with the knower. This would be impossible for a being absolutely devoid of action.

Among medieval thinkers we find the constant use of the principle *agere sequitur esse* ("action flows out of being"). As a being acts, so it is in itself; and vice versa, as a being is, so it acts. If, for instance, a man is kind or cruel by temperament, his actions will be continuous with that temperament and reveal that temperament. We have sayings that point to the same insight, such as, "nothing succeeds like success," failure tends to breed more of its kind, etc., a pattern in human living the English philosopher John Stuart Mill (1806-1873) was moved to write on in his later years as one of life's lessons.

> It is one of nature's general rules and part of her habitual injustice that "to him that hath shall be given, but from him that hath not shall be taken even that which he hath" (Matt. 25:29). The ordinary and predominant tendency of good is toward more good. Health, strength, knowledge, wealth, virtue are not only good in themselves but facilitate and promote the acquisition of good, both of the same and of other kinds. The person who can learn easily is he who already knows much; it is the strong and not the sickly person who can do everything which most conduces to health. Those who find it easy to gain money are not the poor but the rich; while health, strength, knowledge, talents are all means of acquiring riches, and riches are often an indispensable means of acquiring these.[2]

One could go on giving reasons for taking a man's actions as the man himself, especially if one were to refine his notion of action to include more than what is merely externally perceived. And yet a little reflection should make one pause before going on with this equating of a man with his actions or deeds. The writings of Marx and the great encyclicals of the popes on labor, for example, both make the point that human labor is not just another marketable commodity but rather an extension of the human personality itself, so that to wrong a person's work is to wrong the person himself, to take away his labor by economic exploitation is to alienate him from his own *human being*. Putting the point as directly as possible: There is *more* to a man than just his deeds. That *more* makes a crucial difference. It is this, in fact, that qualifies for "self," and not one's deeds.

Consider a moment. Don't deeds redound on the man? Deeds shape a man's being, don't they? And can't this shaping be for better or for worse? A man successful in the eyes of his fellowman is not necessarily a good man, is he? How many times have acclaimed leaders in a community been unmasked, shown to be worthy of contempt? Contrariwise, a man who fails repeatedly before the world is by no means thereby a failure in himself, is he? Naturally the desirable combination is success and goodness together. A man's successes should not "turn his head," should not make him into an arrogant, power-conscious, and self-centered individual. What does this prove, if not that deeds and the self are separable? That it is the man himself resulting from the deeds who is more significant than his deeds? Indeed failures, when they give rise to a beautiful character, help make a man that much more lovable. Clearly then, deeds and the self can't be equated without qualification.

What is that qualification? Why is it true, *in some sense*, that actions are the man himself? We saw how an absolutely inert being is inconceivable. To that extent, therefore, a man's self must be continuous, not separate, from his actions. If nothing else, certainly the man himself is continuous with his action of choosing how to "take," what to make of his successes and failures. This intermediate act of choosing how to shape himself through his actions is, as we shall see, precisely what we should understand as the man himself.

Perhaps, too, there is another qualification, one related to our remarks on human labor as not just another object or commodity. To have, to possess objects, is to act, is it not? And to a certain extent this action of *having* coincides with *being*? Obviously. Without the minimum goods and health necessary, a man would cease to exist. On the other hand, it is also clear that merely *having* is not enough either. Many of us live and have, and yet complain that we have not really had the chance to *be* ourselves. Granted, the "chance" to be really oneself is a relative thing. After all, with almost nothing, the biblical Job was still always himself. Ordinarily, though, living and merely surviving are not coincident with *being* oneself. We agree then that one needs *to have enough* in order to really be oneself, but that wherever the relative point of having enough is located for any given individual's circumstances in life, at that point being and having coincide.[3] At that point, oneself and one's actions overlap. Our previous point of distinguishing actions from being oneself, therefore, referred to actions beyond this coincident point of being and having.

But are we not in effect holding that there is already a self, namely, the coincident, overlapping point of *being* and *having*, before there can be a self? Did we not say that the man himself is shaped by his deeds, by which we meant deeds beyond this overlapping point? How can there be a self before there can be a self?

Let us note, first of all, that the problem of self does not occur in subhumans. It arises, as we noted, only in humans, and then only when they reflect, turn back in on themselves to sort out the various candidates for the self. We saw how one then eventually asks: is the self already there among the plurality in man, merely waiting to be discovered and singled out? Or is the human self yet to *become*? Or is the self both being and becoming at once? It will not do to say that the self does not exist at all now, but merely *becomes*. This would be saying on the one hand that it issues out of nothingness, and on the other hand that it never issues out, since as *becoming* it is always at any given point *not yet*. Are we then forced to say that the self already exists, even though in merely inchoate form? If we admit this, we would in effect also admit that *becoming* then means only quantitative additional growth, accretion, increase. This hardly seems correct in speaking of humans who constantly decide and fashion themselves qualitatively to be this or that *kind* of a man. And it sometimes happens, as in the case of Martin Luther, that a man repudiates all that he ever was to "start a new leaf." Clearly, the problem of the self has forced us back to the point which one thinker formulated as love's imperative for all men; namely, "BECOME WHAT THOU ART."⁴ What could such an imperative, that combines both being and becoming, mean?

2 CONNECTION TO ETHICS

The new word "imperative" alerts us to the relation the problem of the self has to the problem of ethics. No matter what ethics book you open, and no matter how divergent the authors of those books may be from one another in their particular conclusions about moral problems, it can be shown that their line of thought to that particular conclusion moved from the *is* to the *ought*. They described a fact, then moved across to prescribe a value. They went from the indicative, factual mood to the imperative mood.

If we were right in holding, then, that to a certain extent a man's actions are continuous with his being, it follows that to command a man to do a certain action with a very explicit idea of connecting that action to his being ("Become what thou art") is to join together the *is* and the *ought* in him. By the same token, isn't this to join the self and those actions at once of *being* and *becoming* in him? These latter, after all, are paraphrases of the is-ought relationship. We are now both at the nub of the ethical problem and at its beginning.

It was the British philosopher David Hume (1711-1776) who gave the classic statement on the gap between the *is* and the *ought* as the nub of ethical thought. In his work A *Treatise of Human Nature*, Hume points out how anyone engaged in ethical discussion usually goes from:

> Observations concerning human affairs . . . to propositions connected with an *ought* or *ought not*. The change is imperceptible, but as this *ought* or *ought not* expresses some new relation, or affirmation, it is necessary that it should be observed and explained.⁵

Why should this gap be explained, since Hume himself admits we do it so naturally? In a sense, philosophy is an attempt to make obvious things visible. To philosophize is to bring to the forefront of one's awareness what otherwise would forever remain implicit and thus unknown to him.[6] The power to move oneself from implicit to explicit awareness is so exclusively human that any such transition is a step toward a higher quality of human existence. Secondly, whatever the self may be, we certainly move toward it whenever we make the effort to break through the limits of our ignorance toward knowledge. Thus Socrates characterized philosophy simply as "self-knowledge." The more self-aware I am, the more of a human being I am. The two are, as we said, profoundly if perplexingly co-related. Here is a clue that whatever the self may be, the activity of awareness, of knowledge, is certainly inseparable from it. We can press harder now as to just why the gap between the *is* and the *ought* is a problem, and how this problem overlaps the problem of self.

Every philosopher asks the question: what is reality? Suppose we grant the Thomistic answer that reality is what *exists*, what *is*. Whatever the content or reference of the moral *ought* may be, it is either not reducible to the *is* (that which exists) or it is so reducible. Either way problems arise. For if the ought does not reduce to what exists, then this can only mean that it refers to what is not real, to nothing. Surely no one wants to hold that all moral striving, which is at the core of human living, no matter how various its forms, is ultimately an illusion and reducible to nothing. Even if we hold that at the end of life everything is absurd, since death is absolute (if so one believes), this is still not the same as saying that our individual acts of moral striving which are so agonizingly real are all about nothing.

Suppose one presses the question and admits that moral striving is indeed real, but that there is nothing beyond the effort itself that is real. In this case, we find ourselves impaled on the other horn of Hume's dilemma. We would in effect be saying that the *ought* refers to something real, and thus to what exists. What is the sense of saying then that what *is* is the same as what *ought* to be? Even as we speak of the *ought*, we point to the future, the continuation of the present beyond itself. We certainly do not mean the *ought* to refer to anything already existing, as though closed in on itself.

Whether we do not reduce the *ought* to the *is*, therefore, or whether we do so reduce it, we seem unable to come out with any believable sense. And yet there is a connection. What? And how to get at it? We saw how the problem of the gap between the *is* and the *ought* coincides with the problem of *being* and *becoming*. We can now recognize both as identical components of the problem of *self*: "Become what thou art." We saw how it does not make sense to say that the self is in no way present at all, at the same time we were forced to say that in man the self is not yet, and only comes-to-be. Clearly, we need to reflect on what we mean when we say that reality is what *is*.

A *Reality as Tendency*

To come-to-be is to come forth, to issue out of something that already *is* into something that *is-not* yet. New things arise from other things, not from absolute nothingness. In the perpetual rhythm of nature, "one death is the parent of a thousand lives" John Henry Newman wrote in *Second Spring*, an artistic statement of the corruption-generation processes in nature. This should lead us to look for the union of being and becoming in a view of reality as *tendential*, a view of every being as inclined to, tending toward, action. Again we recall how an absolutely inert being is impossible. To *be*, then, is to tend toward acting and interacting with other beings who themselves are tendential, and thus related to other beings in the universe.[7]

We see now how the gap Hume points out between the *is* and the *ought* appears insoluble only if the *is* is rigorously restricted to a static in-itself view of being. No being is that way, if to be is truly to *tend toward* others. To tend is to transcend, to go beyond its limits at the same time that a being *is*. This is the coincident point of the *is* and the *ought*. A being that tends beyond itself straddles, so to speak, both areas of *being* and *becoming*, the *is* and the *ought*, fact and value.

If we reflect further, we will note how this going beyond one's own self-containment through action and interaction with other beings can take several forms. Living beings tend to interact with others differently than inanimate beings interact with others. There is more breaking of limits when living beings assimilate and reproduce others, over and above such acts as physically contacting or coinciding with each other, chemically dissolving into each other, etc. There is, for instance, a breaking of limits through consciousness of other beings in one's immediate environment. This is "assimilation" no longer on the physical but on the "intentional" level of consciousness, a much more free-wheeling assimilation in which neither the subject nor object of consciousness is physically altered. Finally, there is a breaking of all limits in an act of intellectual consciousness that assimilates not only any and all beings around it but is completely self-reflective. For an intellectual being can know itself in the act of knowing its objects, in one and the same action. With this power of self-reflection, an intellectual being can "intend" not only the things around it but its own actions, indeed its own being, including even the *limits* of its actions and its own being, a remarkable instance of breaking *all* limits. Why? Because to be aware of a limit is already to be beyond that limit. When I know my limit, I am by that token beyond it. How?

A man, because of this power of self-reflection, is able to differentiate himself from other beings precisely as a man, and from other men precisely as *this* or *that* individual man. More, he can know his own ignorance—what he knows, and what he does not know—thereby escaping in a way the limits of his own ignorance, and thus being open to all there may be to know. He can be aware of his desires, and hence desire to desire those things he does not actually desire now, showing again the presence of "transcendence," of going beyond his limit through his desires. In short, when we come to consider man, we find a being with a tendency toward, an inclination to, *all* things through self-reflection. We seem to be closing in now on that point in man which holds being and nonbeing together, hence on the concept of self, through this peculiarly human power of transcendence.

B *Human Tendency*

We have seen how there is a continuity between being and acting, how we must *have* certain actions and things in order to be really ourselves. It is this really *being ourselves*, reinforcing that coincident point for *being-becoming* and *ought* and *having* all viewed as tendential being, that we are now trying to tie together. How are we to understand tendential being in man? In a word, what actions do men tend toward that specifically single them out precisely as men? Is it not human consciousness, the peculiar power to know *all* things, revealed in that same power's ability to turn in on itself and realize its own limits, thereby paradoxically transcending those limits at any given point in its "stock" of knowledge? To repeat: to be aware of one's ignorance is to be already beyond that ignorance, inasmuch as one is alerted to it and to that extent already on his way out of it toward additional knowledge. Similarly, to know this or that object and at the same time to know you know that object is already to be beyond that subject-object relationship, since you are able to watch it, to penetrate it in seeking to understand it. Through reflective consciousness you are outside at the same time that you are inside the subject-object relation of your act of knowing.

Whether the mind moves extensively then to object after object in a field of knowledge in seemingly endless succession, or whether it moves intensively toward an understanding in depth of its own nature as consciousness in relation to those objects, it is always able to go beyond its limits at any given situation. Is this not an infinity of sorts? Even to argue, for instance, that our minds are bound within their various limited perspectives of interpretation is to be able to view those perspectives from "beyond" them all; else the statement, which is an overview, would be impossible. Hence, as Aristotle noted, "the mind is in a way all things." This is man's impressive power which, as we shall see, Aristotle and Plato designated as "the man himself." For it is the mind, in its tendency toward all things, that seems to combine within itself being and becoming at once. Its very being is to become, to be open to all things. It is, at the same time that it is not yet, being and becoming together.

And yet, a closer look at the thought of Plato and Aristotle on this point shows that though we may indeed be on the right track in focusing on the mind as the focus of the man himself, we have not yet gone far enough. For when Plato and Aristotle talked of the man himself as his intellect, they invariably related it to moral goodness. They talked of the intellect as a directing force (even though they did not clearly distinguish intellect from will), a governor of all else that is in man, to the highest point of moral goodness. A comprehensive collection of texts on the self in Plato and Aristotle is not our aim here nor is such really necessary. It should be sufficient for our purpose simply to highlight their thought that the mind is and ought to be the governor of all that is in man, and then to reflect on the implications of this ambivalent concept of the mind as an aid to our own search for the self.

c The Self as Ruler Principle

We need recall only three of various dramatic passages in Plato to show the notion of directing mind as Plato's idea of the really real man. The allegory of the cave[8] is too well-known to have its details repeated here. Suffice it to say that in that Platonic myth the prisoner who does break away from his fellow prisoners and the shadows on the wall is differentiated from them precisely by his *initial decision* to break away, by his *sustained decision* to go through the passage to the mouth of the cave and out to the fields and trees in the sunlight, and by his *final decision* to come back and tell his fellow prisoners all about the difference between the real things he saw in the sunlight and the shadows on the wall they believe to be real.

In the gradations of knowledge and classes of men in the same work, deterministic though the context be, we find Plato again making the same point. The philosopher, the man who *knows*, who is the epitome of human reality, *rules*. He makes the key decisions. Why precisely he? Because he knows the good and *is* thereby himself *good*. This point must be stressed. It is not mere knowledge of the good (as is usually said) but rather the inseparability of *knowing* the good and *being* good in Plato's thought that qualifies the philosopher-king to rule, to make the decision.

The same point is brought out in the *Phaedrus*, where man is represented as the charioteer *driving* his steeds toward the fullness of vision, and then back again to share his vision with his friend. Lastly, a dramatic presentation is given in the sixth theory of love in the *Symposium*. Love is shown to be a mediating force that propels the mind to ascend to the highest point, from where it sees everything in the fullness of its source. Unlike the two previous illustrations, there is no return of the seer and no sharing of the vision in this passage, so it might appear that this is a case simply of knowing the good. Yet the concluding passage of Socrates' magnificent discourse is all of a piece really with the two previous illustrations. For Socrates concludes with these words to Phaedrus that reveal how Plato's thought goes beyond mere possession of knowledge toward *decision*.

Such, Phaedrus—and I speak not only to you, but to all of you—were the words of Diotima; and I am persuaded of their truth. And *being persuaded of them I try to persuade others*, that in the attainment of this end human nature will not easily find a helper better than love. And therefore, also, I say that every man ought to honor him as I myself honor him, and walk in his ways, and exhort others to do the same, and praise the power and spirit of love according to the measure of my ability now and forever [Italics added].[9]

In Aristotle, we find the position on who the man himself is embedded in his discussion of human friendship.[10] Friendship is of three sorts: one, based on use of the other person; another, based on pleasure from the other person; and a third, based on *the man himself* as against what he can do or produce for the other. And who is this man himself on whom genuine friendship rests? Aristotle's reply is clear-cut:

> Just as a city or any other systematic whole is most properly identified with the most authoritative element in it, so is a man; and therefore, the man who loves this and gratifies it is most of all a lover of self. Besides, a man is said to have or not have self-control according as his reason has or has not the control, on the assumption that this is the *man himself*: and the things men have done on a rational principle are thought most properly their own acts and voluntary acts. That this is the man himself then, or is so more than anything else, is plain; and also that the good man loves most this part of him [Italics added].[11]

Where this text occurs, Aristotle shows that a man cannot be a friend to others in the third kind of friendship (the only genuine friendship, by analogy to which the other two are called "friendships") unless he is first of all a friend to himself. A man, then, must first love himself before he can love others.

There are three sorts of self-love Aristotle mentions here. There is a universal love of self in men, which shows itself in the fact that no man really wants to be another man. Indeed, we always imagine our own selves in those others we imagine we would like to be! This self-love is not the basis for genuine friendship. Neither is the second type, which is immoral selfishness, self-centeredness in relation to others. Rather, the genuine type of self-love is the reaffirmation of what a man himself is. And what is that? This brings us back to the problem of self.

Aristotle, in the text cited above, clearly states that the man himself is the life of reason in him, his foremost principle, just as the head of state is the foremost principle. A man who loves himself imposes self-control, the control of reason over all his other members, like a well-integrated political unity. This prevalence of the life of reason in him is what a virtuous man loves. This is authentic self-love, the basis for genuine friendship. When such a man sees the life of reason in others, he merely recognizes himself and thereby loves those others in genuine friendship. Hence to love the other *for himself* is really to recognize in the other an *alter ego*, another I. All friends thus love one thing similarly present in them all, the life of reason that is "the man himself."

Such briefly is Aristotle's thought on human friendship and the self. Look at this position closely. Isn't there a similarity here with Plato's position insofar as Aristotle explicitly identifies the "self" with the "ruler," the element in man which *controls* through "desiring deliberation and deliberating desire"? Accordingly, not mere intellectual knowledge, but beyond that the principle of decision, choice, government, rule, is the principle in man identified by Plato and Aristotle as "the man himself." How does this, then, relate to the tendential view of being we looked at in the previous section?

3 THE SELF AS FREE: PROPOSED ANSWER

As a being is, so it acts. There is a continuity between being and action. Aquinas, from whom we largely derive this doctrine, repeatedly says: *esse est tendere*.[12] To be is to be tendential. Being and action are proportionate, that is, actions are mediated by the "form," the kind of being that each being is. Following Aristotle, Aquinas points out that the peculiarity of man is his ability to receive all forms, not physically, but intentionally in the mind. He is, through his mind, all things.

What does this mean in the light of inclination or tendency to follow being or form? It seems clear that if all forms can be present in man, man can then incline toward any and all forms present in him through knowledge. To incline toward all the forms present in him, however, is not yet to choose among them. The "ruler" principle in man must come into play precisely in this act of choosing among all the things that he knows, in selecting that particular one to which he will connect himself in desire. Choosing that one, he rejects the rest. And so, finally, we come to focus on the particular principle in man that seems to qualify best as the *self*, namely, the principle of free choice in man. But it will be necessary, at this point, to linger a bit on the idea of freedom.

In talking of freedom, we are talking of an act of the will. A person wills something when he inclines toward something known as good, as desirable. To be unwilling, obversely, is to decline away from an object known as not good, not desirable. It is clear that if we knew only one object and knew that object only as good, we would *necessarily* incline toward that object. We could, quite literally, not help but will that object. And if there were only one way to attain that object and we knew that way, it is also clear that we would necessarily will that way. In such a case there would be no freedom. Freedom arises when we know something as good, and, without adverting to anything not-good about it, perceive many means of attaining that good. Our freedom plays on the field of means toward an end seen as simply good, that is to say, without adverting to anything that may be undesirable about that end.

From this we see how such various sayings as "the truth shall make you free," "knowledge is power," "to know is always better than not to know," etc., articulate the necessary relationship between knowing and willing. My freedom can only be as wide as my awareness and knowledge of the field of my choice, that is to say, the knowledge I have at the time of the various means available to me of attaining the end willed. Furthermore, even that end itself, which at one time I necessarily will, can still be made an object of freedom by viewing it, if I can, as a means to something further, which I then will as my further end now. Let's see if we can translate this into concrete illustrations.

Suppose I am a penniless fellow and it strikes me, after scanning possibilities open to me, that what I want most of all in life is lots of money. At that point, viewing lots of money simply as good and not adverting to any of the evil things money may bring, I cannot but will lots of money. My desire cleaves to money without vacillation. Of course there are usually many ways to gain lots of money. So I am free within the field of play of these various means to the end: gambling, hard work, studying for a well-paying degree, marrying a rich mate, cultivating the proverbial rich old uncle who never married and now gives signs in his waning days of wavering in the matter of selecting his heir, etc. On this field of means known to me, I am not "necessitated." I am free to choose, to *consent* to any one of them. Why? Precisely because of this plurality, in which each one of these plural means is seen only as a partial good, *one* way of getting what I want. The others will do also. None of them is necessary, therefore; all of them are contingent. Aquinas puts this point clearly:

> We are masters of our own actions by reason of our being able to choose this or that. But choice regards not the end, but the means to the end, as is said in *Nicomachean Ethics*, III, 2, 111b-27. Consequently, the desire of the ultimate end is not among those actions of which we are masters.[13]

And again:

> But man acts from judgment, because by this cognitive power he judges that something should be avoided or sought. But because this judgment, in the case of some particular act, is not from a natural instinct, but from some act of comparison in the reason, therefore he acts from free judgment and retains the power of being inclined to various alternatives.[14]

Another illustration is given in a *Feiffer* series of cartoons with these successive captions: "I thought school was a jail until I got a job. Boy, was that a jail! / Then I got married. Even more of a jail! / Until I got drafted into the army. The worst jail yet! / Until I got in trouble and went to jail—; And learned that jail is even more of a jail than school, a job, marriage, or the army. / So finally I know what freedom is all about: the right *to choose which jail.*"

We can see now how the questions of the self, of *being* and *becoming*, of the *is* and the *ought*, of unity and plurality, really all point us to the power of free choice in man, their locus of convergence. Whether we take Plato's and Aristotle's concept of "the man himself" as the ruler principle, or Aquinas' view of being as tendential, we see why the power of free choice, the power that shapes a man into the kind of man he is, seems to be the best candidate for the *self*. So it is, as Aristotle points out, that we do not take people as fully themselves when they are behaving wildly and without control. They are "beside themselves," we say. No, "the man himself" is that *ruling* principle of free choice, which through its reflective power shapes the subject who is the man himself. By this we do not mean to make some sort of substance out of something that is merely one of man's actions. It is a question, rather, of fixing on a *principle* in man that we can accept as the man himself. Later, we shall take up the continuity of this principle with other principles in man.

In all other beings with which we are familiar, natural tendencies are mechanistic. René Descartes (1596-1650) well observed that animals are really in a sense still machines, though more complicated ones than plants and inorganic things.[15] Only in man does the natural proportionate tendency *to be* and *to act* point toward nothing specific, since it is open to everything the mind can present to it—and the mind, as the breaker of all limits including its own, is open to all things. Thus man *is* indeed; he is a human *being*. This means, however, becoming what I choose to be. The power of free choice is therefore "the man himself"; it is at once what is both being and becom-

ing, subject (the chooser) and object (what is shaped), the result of choice and the choosing power. In fact it seems sensible
to hold that the real self in me is what I have made, what I
have chosen myself to be up to this moment. In this sense it is
true, as Freudians say, that we are walking structures of our
past. We *are* our free will as habituated to choose up to now,
whether virtuously or otherwise. And at the very heart of this
habituated power there remains always the possibility of repudiating its whole self, of being radically other than it is now
and starting on a wholly new pattern. In this sense, as Jean-
Paul Sartre (1905–) put it well, nothingness can be said to lie
at the core of being human.[16] But at this point perhaps we
should go back and pose the problem of self in more detail, to
see whether this answer we have advanced will bear analysis.

4 FURTHER EXPLANATIONS

The problem of self arises because of the cleft in human
consciousness that enables man to recognize a plurality within
him vying for the title of self. It is this reflective consciousness
in man that formulates reflexive forms of discourse such as the
intensive "Lady Macbeth did the deed herself" or the reflexive
"Lady Macbeth hurt herself in the process of murdering Dun-
can." The problem of the self is apparent here from the fact
that we can inquire which *self* Lady Macbeth hurt:

(1) her physical person, such as skin, flesh, organism?
(2) her psychological state, whether this be the conscious
or subconscious or both?
(3) her moral condition, in the sense of Plato's axiom that
wrongdoing is its own worst punishment since a person
becomes bad by his bad deed?

We have been saying it is the moral sense of the self that
best identifies the man himself. Everything else in man is
relative to this self, and the opening sentences of Kant's *Fundamental Principles of the Metaphysics of Morals* are very pertinent here:

Nothing can possibly be conceived in the world, or even out of it, which can be called good without qualification, except a *good will*. Intelligence, wit, judgment, and the other talents of the mind, however they may be named, are undoubtedly good and desirable in many respects; but these gifts of nature may also become extremely bad and mischievous if the will which is to make use of them, and which therefore constitutes what is called character, is not good. Power, riches, honor, even health, and the general well-being and contentment with one's condition which is called happiness, inspire pride, and often presumption, if there is not a good will to correct the influence of these on the mind, and with this also to rectify the whole principle of acting and adapt it to its end.[17]

Nothing, not even a brilliant intellect, makes a good man except a good will. We see better now why the question of self coincides with the question of morals. Whatever other meaning of self one propounds, whether it be a self swallowed up in the Absolute (as in Spinoza and Hegel) or in the collectivity (as in Marx), whether it be a self propounded as authenticating itself in breaking away from the crowd (as in Nietzsche, Kierkegaard, Marcel, Buber, et al.) or acting a role within the herd (as in Goffman and other contemporary psychologists), in the last analysis we note that these are all subsequent developments to the crucial decisive principle in man—free choice—which initiates and sustains, or repudiates as the case may be, the process of the individual becoming more and more himself.

The obvious objection, of course, is that the man himself is precisely that—the whole man—since this is the only being in itself and all the rest are merely his actions. Why go through all this nit-picking about various "candidates" in man? But the difficulty with this objection is that it really proves too much and thus nothing about the self. For our problem arises precisely because in that "whole man" we find a variety of principles and various manifestations of seemingly various personalities. Thus to simply point back to the whole man in which this plurality is contained solves nothing. Precision is necessary.

On the other hand, once foiled in the whole man approach, if one resorts to parts (v.g., hand in Hegel, face in Levinas, reason in Aristotle, etc.), as we seemed to have done above, we are also beset with difficulties. For, to paraphrase St. Paul, one part cannot say to another part "I do not need you." The plurality in man conspires toward a whole functioning unity. One life is present in all of the parts, though of course, as the medievals used to say, that one life is not wholly present in any one part. Up to a certain point, dismemberment can happen without loss of life. It is to this living principle in man by which everything in him is alive and is human that we must look, therefore, if we are to get a sensible focus on the self. In death, the absence of this living principle leaves the "human"

Self
- Passive principles that cannot possibly be the man himself
  1 Physical, material, bodily components.
  2 Passive intellect, not as in Aristotle but as memory bank/deposit.
  3 Passive will: Will willed, as habituated=stable character="person."
- Active (conscious) principle in man
  4 Subconscious.
  5 Intellectual consciousness, v.g., ruler in Plato and Aristotle.
  6 Will consciousness:
     We desire, and desire not to or to desire;
     we choose, and choose not to or to choose; thus showing the ultimate reflexivity of the will on itself.

remains no longer truly a human being; so, too, there is a correlative sense in which we can talk of this living principle as *active* vis-à-vis activated, passive principles. Let's not mistake this, however, as a "ghost in the machine" view of man. But with that caution, perhaps we can diagram (see page 30) the correlatively passive and active principles as follows, beginning with the unlikely candidates for the self and moving toward the precise principle of free choice that we have already settled on as the man himself. Beginning at the top of the diagram, let's take up each point briefly with an eye to narrowing down the man himself to the active, conscious principle of free choice, the ruler principle.

Number 1 in the diagram, the physical, material, bodily components of man, whether as individual parts or as a whole, will not do as the self for the obvious reasons we have already pointed out in one way or another in previous sections. The mocking tone in which we talk of a person simply "lusting for the body" of another captures this point concretely.

Number 2 in the diagram, the intellect as passive or as a simple memory bank, will not do either. For while it is true that a man who does not remember his past (as in a case of total amnesia) is not truly himself, it is not simply the retention of one's past but the recognition of them precisely as past and as mine that is vital to being the man himself. And this is the classic answer to Hume's statement of the problem of the self. It is *I* who bond, who remember my states of consciousness as *mine*. Moreover, on occasion we say, "I remember now. I was wrong when I recalled that to you." This shows a prior principle to memory, a principle that itself controls and corrects memory.[18] Of the two, it is this active intellectual principle that would be the better candidate for the self, for without it the memories would not be memories. Why not stay with this as the self? Because, to repeat, a brilliant intellect, an intellect at its best, does not necessarily make a good man; indeed it can be employed toward proportionately greater evil.[19]

Number 3, the will as passive. We mean here the pattern of habits of willing a person has developed. Why not call this the self? We do in fact include this in the notion of the self we proposed, for the habitual will-acts of a man are constitutive of the man himself. But this needs further precision, since it is always possible for a person to repudiate with one act of the will all he has ever been—an extraordinary feat, to be sure, but not impossible.[20] The will, like the intellect, in reflecting upon itself is ever transcendent of its limits, including even its own habitual patterns. That is why we preferred to focus the self within the will itself, rather than on habitual patterns which may be present at a given time.

Number 4, the subconscious, seems at first to be a good candidate for the man himself. From the time of Sigmund Freud (1856-1939), psychoanalysts have shown beyond doubt that many of our manifest actions are rooted in and controlled by our hidden subconscious desires, fears, frustrations, etc. What we are, then, in this reckoning, would be our subconscious inclinations and experiential residues, whether these be reducible ultimately to one pleasure principle or to a cluster of archaeological relics from our ancestors. In either case, the subconscious as the man himself would be thought of as the true directing force behind all our conscious and open motivations.

The last sentence, however, gives the very reason why we can't accept the subconscious as the man himself. How can the directing principle, not conscious of itself (in this supposition), be the man himself when, as we saw, a man without self-control is really beside himself? To say the subconscious is conscious of itself but precisely within its own context of subconsciousness is the kind of nonsense Freud himself repudiated in the face of mockery from his fellow scientists, who raised this point against the "subconscious" when Freud pioneered with the idea. Secondly, Freudians themselves will tell you the subconscious is certainly not the ruling principle we are seeking, since in all cases of "maturity" in the Freudian context the subconscious itself is submitted and adjusted to the reality principle by the ego. Indeed, that is the substance of the Freudian concept of maturity as "the ability to postpone gratification": the reality principle, the ego, forces the subconscious, the pleasure principle, to trim its demands to what the actual situation will allow. Thus:

From	*To*
Immediate satisfaction	Delayed satisfaction
Pleasure	Restraint of pleasure
Joy (play)	Toil (work)
Receptiveness (the characteristic of the animistic-narcissistic and parent attachment-religious stage of mankind)	Productiveness (the characteristic of the scientific, mature stage of mankind)
Absence of repression	Security

It is clear from the above that the final ruling principle is not the subconscious, but the crucial "reality principle." Hence Herbert Marcuse (1898–), from whom we borrow this chart, writes: "This part and this part alone is to set the objectives, the norms, and values of the ego; as *reason*, it becomes the sole repository of judgement, truth, rationality; it decides what is useful and useless, good and evil."[21] And along the same vein, Peter Homans writes:

> Taking our cue from the rather central notion of metapsychology, we must say that structurally the Freudian self is "an awareness beset by instinct and culture." Freudian man lives at the juncture "of instinct and culture." When fully developed, the Freudian self is a unity of instincts and psychic apparatus, each divided further into ego, id, and superego on the one hand, and into the life and death instincts on the other hand.[22]

We might say then that in Freud, too, the self is finally pinpointed to a balanced tension in man of all the restless forces within him, when submitted to reason (*logos*) and to external necessity (*ananke*). One need only look at the chart, however, to see that "reason" here, with its whole set of psychoanalytic universe of discourse, is altogether a diverse term from Aristotle's "reason." There *is* an overlap in the two positions, however, in the assignment of some "ruler" in man as the self.

Number 5, intellectual consciousness, needs little further elaboration, since we have discussed this in our texts from Plato, Aristotle, and Kant.

Number 6, the will as reflexively conscious. This is the principle we have pinpointed as the man himself. Our final task is to deal with some objections against this position.

1 One can object, for instance, that no matter what principle in man we select as the self, we find ourselves objectifying it even in looking at it, thus vitiating our intuition that the self is a subject. My answer would be that the will, just like the intellect, has a certain power of reflection upon itself that enables it to be completely present to its own actions simultaneously, without a further act trailing off into an infinite regress. In other words, we (1) desire and simultaneously either (2) desire not to or (3) desire to desire what we are desiring. We may continue our act of desiring or we can break it off—with effort perhaps, even with heroic effort, but we *can*. The point is that it is possible in the act of desiring something for that very same act *of desiring* to turn for or against itself. Thus the intellect's power to be subject-object at once in regard to itself through complete self-presence in reflection is also true of the will. The will is, after all, intellectual appetite.

2 Another objection might be that it is absurd to take just one part of the man as the man himself. On this point William James has written: "As Aristotle writes and Hegel loves to quote, an amputated hand is not even a hand."[23] In other words, the totality, not the part, is the reality. In reply, we may note that an amputated "hand" is cut off and away from the man himself. In pinpointing the self as free will, we not only mean no isolation of this sort but in fact take the will precisely as conjoined to everything in man that is not the will. The will is clearly "conjoined" to the intellect, for it can will nothing

except what is known.[24] But intellectual thought itself is "continued," through the image in the imagination (phantasm), to all the organs of sensation. And the organs of sensation are sustained by the vegetative powers in man, and there is thus a continuity, not an isolation, with everything else in man that is not the will, when we focus on the will as the man himself.

But isn't this in effect falling back on the whole man after all, a position we already rejected? No, because it is a question of *primacy* here: Which principle, among the many present in man, best qualifies as the focus of the man himself? We can only agree that any position on the self that does not somehow hold the totality of the individual to itself is unacceptable.

3 Finally, someone may argue that the free will is really controlled by the further principle of the subconscious—and indeed by many other unknown but determining influences on one's life. Such an objection, however, is really not against our position of the will as the self, but rather against the presence of any freedom in man at all. This is a vast subject, entirely beyond our scope here.[25] Suffice it to say that we here are talking of means *known* to a desired end as the proper field of freedom. Until any of these subconscious and supposedly "determining" elements enter into that area of consciousness and intellectual awareness, it is not, in our terms, fair material for the formation of the self. Moreover, it seems impossible to talk of unknown elements in a man, beyond his control, as constitutive of the man himself.[26] In any case, it seems clear that a conscious and free awareness is a necessary constituent of the self.

In summary we can say that it is the free and reflexive will in man that is "the man himself" toward which his actions, his performances beyond the coincident point of being and having, redound. That free will is an actuality in him, but it is a peculiar actuality in that its whole inclination is toward becoming what it chooses to be. It is the juncture point, therefore, of being and becoming; of the *is* and the *ought*; in a sense, even of nothingness and being. We find this juncture only in man. Everything else subhuman seems to move in quantitative, mechanical, deterministic—and often unknown—ways. In man, however, no self can be predicated until the "ruler" in him acts. Yet neither can this "ruler" in man act without intellectual awareness of its field of choices. Hence, much of the burden of human living lies in trying to see the various possibilities really open to choice in any given situation. What it is we really want in life is not always too easy a question. "The cloud that hangs over us of our possibilities is the self" as someone has written.[27]

And that brings us to our next topic. For to be interested at all in choosing what sort of a man to become among the possibilities open to me, I must already have decided that life is worth living; that becoming a certain self is worth my life's efforts. What is that certain self one aims for? There are probably as many answers as there are individual desires and ambitions: money, family security, power, public and social acceptance, friends, etc. All these, though, are beside the point. We are asking whether there is a recognizable goal which can be seen beyond all these immediate goals, toward which the free tendency in man processes itself into being. What, in other words, is life all about—viewed in as ultimate a perspective as one is able to grasp?

THE MEANING OF LIFE
AS WHOLING

From this chapter onward, we will trace out the idea of love as a wholing process as it has appeared in certain major stages of western thought. The principal point throughout the rest of this book will be that this conception of love as the impulsion of the fragment toward the whole is the key to the problems of the self and the meaning-of-life question which, as we have seen, are merely two different aspects of the very same reality.

We will trace out in a general way the dialectical contrasts between (1) the ancient Greek idea of love as a wholing process, with man as the center; and (2) the medieval Christian tradition of kenotic love, *agape*, with the center of love shifted by faith to the One Absolute, God. The brevity of these two sections will in a way be compensated for by the lengthy and specific treatment of (3) the Lutheran-Catholic dialogue on the meaning of disinterested love in a Christian context. Finally, we will touch on (4) the recent Christian idea of love in Kierkegaard and Bonhoeffer as representing the shift toward the contemporary interest in searching for God within oneself, within time and memory.

1 THE GREEK IDEA OF LOVE

The idea of love as a sort of wholing goes all the way back to the pre-Socratic philosopher Empedocles. He held that the various comings and goings in nature, the ups and downs in individual destinies, the rhythmic and a-rhythmic variations in cosmic occurrences were all ultimately traceable either to the unitive influence of Love or the disruptive influence of Strife as each predominated alternately with the other in the world. He thought of Love and Strife as gods, complete with shape and position, with Love gathered to a sphere in the cosmic center (rest, unity, harmony) and Strife spread in an even layer all over the outer surface of that sphere. These two were both under "oath" or necessity in their endless *dine* ("whirl"), a to-ing and fro-ing of dominance and defeat. Besides the "major alternations" of prevalence and recession, there was a "minor alternation" of speed and slowness, in terms of an ever-increasing speed striving to reach total speed and victory with the elements fully separated and Love forced to the center.

"Without delay," the opposite world of increasing Love would then begin moving outward from the center and binding the totally separated elements into all sorts of fantastic mixtures on their way to "final" union into whole-natured forms as they were blissfully assumed into the sphere. And so on, in an eternal cycle. Somewhere in this cycle was the "golden age of religion, remote from the present world, of bloodless sacrifices, where beasts are tame," an other-worldliness within a fully philosophical system.

Our world with all its various combinations Empedocles saw as falling into the period of increasing Strife. As time went on, different parts of our bodies would be torn into separate pieces and would cling together in monstrous combinations. "Then separate limbs will wander disconsolately about the world on the eve of the dissolution of all things into four separate elements." After this catastrophe the world of increasing

Love will begin. The same events will now be repeated in the same order.[1]

Here we meet the original notion of love as a force gathering fragments toward a unity. It is the answer we propose in this book to the problem of the self and the meaning of life. And it is this idea of love as a wholing process that one meets again and again among thinkers through the ages, though of course in varying universes of discourse. So it will help to recall in brief compass the historical highlights of this idea.

We have already touched on love in Plato and Aristotle in the preceding chapter. Here we need only point up the idea of *wholing* in both those philosophers' ideas on love. We see, for example, in the fourth of the six theories of love presented in Plato's *Symposium*, love as a force seeking its original wholeness which somehow it has lost. Sometimes called the Aristophanic myth, the fourth theory is this:

> Original human nature was not like the present; the sexes were not two as they are now, but originally three in number: man, woman, and the union of the two. This third sex once existed and had a name which was lost, so that now "androgeny" is used only as a term of reproach. Primeval man was round, his back and sides forming a circle. He had four hands and four feet, one head with two faces looking opposite ways—four ears, two privy members, etc.[2]

The myth narrates how this breed of men was of terrible might and how, in their insolence, they attacked the gods. As punishment, Zeus cut them in two, right down the middle, gave a twist or two to the parted skin and tied it into a knot at the center, which now appears as the navel. The pairs still clung to each other in a consuming desire for their original unity. As a result of the disruption of their original pairing, they were dying from hunger and self-neglect. It was then that Zeus invented sexual intercourse to save the human race from extinction. Ever since, *every man has roamed forth in search of his other half*. When a pair chance on each other, an amazing friendship blazes forth which "does not appear to be the desire of lover's intercourse but which the soul of either evidently desires and cannot tell, and of which she has only a dark and doubtful presentiment."[3] The wholing process is again underscored in the concluding words of the myth:

> I believe that if our loves were perfectly accomplished, and each one returning to his primeval nature had his original true love, then our race would be happy.[4]

Reading this myth today, one is struck by its imaginative development from Empedocles' thought and, even more significantly, by its rich suggestions about the many mysteries we encounter in our own experiences of love.

In Aristotle we saw how true love consists in loving the life of reason or virtue in myself, and how I am thereby enabled to love another who has the same life of virtue present in him as an *alter ego*, another I. Here again we can observe the similarity of thought between one's "other half" in the *Symposium*, and a friend as an *alter ego* in Aristotle, and prior to both, Empedocles' idea of love as wholing. Says Aristotle:

> Since each of these characteristics belongs to the good man in relation to himself, and he is related to his friend as to himself (for his friend is another self), friendship too is thought to be one of these attributes, and those who have these attributes to be friends. Whether there is or is not friendship between a man and himself is a question we may dismiss for the present; there would seem to be friendship insofar as he is two or more, to judge from the aforementioned attributes of friendship, and from the fact that the extreme of friendship is likened to one's love for oneself.[5]

2 MEDIEVAL IDEAS OF LOVE

From these quick sketches of Greek ideas on love, we skip now to the Middle Ages in order to see how the notion of love as a wholing process received a radical shift in meaning. From the Greek notion of love and friendship (often termed *eros* and *philia*) with man as its center, we find the ages of faith and the age of great cathedrals of Europe wrestling with a kenotic, God-centered idea of love as charity, *agape*.

For the Christian community of those times, God's kenotic love for man revealed itself literally in everything around him. Faith taught that God, the infinite fullness of Being himself, without losing anything and standing to gain absolutely nothing for himself, nevertheless willed creatures into being. This was an infinite gain of sorts for finite man, who as finite was devoid of existence in himself and therefore was willed from *nothingness into actuality*. Furthermore, God gave man all creation for his use. These positions are almost inconceivable to a nonbeliever, perhaps, but one has to try and relive this view in his imagination to see how, for the medieval mind, all of creation was an impressive sacrament of God's unselfish love for men.

Not only did God give himself unselfishly in creation, but the idea was made concrete once and for all when the Godhead emptied himself, as it were (hence "kenotic," from the Greek word *kenosis*, "emptying"), and became enfleshed in Christ; emptied himself, so faith taught, all the way until there was nothing left of self to give—on the cross, for unregenerate men.[6] All over Europe one sees the tremendous impact this doctrine had in the very beautiful records of human response to the crucified Christ through architecture, painting, and heroic attempts to imitate Christ's life, etc. The ideal was to respond to God's love in the way God first had loved them, that is to say, in a totally unselfish love. The "Great Commandment," to love God with one's whole being without remainder and everything else only in reference to God, was all of a piece with their faith.

In the *City of God*, St. Augustine called this Christian attitude of loving all things only in God as the center of them all, *amor rectus*. Sin, on the other hand, was loving creatures without this further reference to God, and therefore Augustine called it *amor curvatus*, love curved away from God and back in on creatures themselves.[7] It is interesting to see how, at its purest, this teaching held that men should love God only for himself, and not so that they might gain happiness or heaven or anything else for themselves. For this would be to loop one's love for all things in God, or even God himself, ultimately back to the individual—the worst form of self-absolutizing, self-idolatry. It was *amor rectus*, then, that was taught and perhaps one of its most beautiful expressions occurred in St. Francis Xavier's hymn of love ("O Deus, Ego Amo Te"), translated as follows by Gerard Manley Hopkins:

O God, I love thee, I love thee—
Not out of hope for heaven for me
Nor fearing not to love and be
In the everlasting burning.
Thou, thou, my Jesus, after me
Didst reach thine arms out dying . . .
And thou couldst see me sinning.

Then I, why should I not love thee,
Not for any gains I see
But just the way that thou didst me
I do love and will love thee.
What must I love thee, Lord, for then?
For being my king and God. Amen.[8]

This poses the problem of disinterested love, which the medievals raised and debated for a long time: Is it really possible to love God with one's whole being without remainder, since this implies loving him without that further looping back toward self-love in any form? To an age of faith it was inconceivable that God should command anything impossible of men. Yet how does one resolve intellectually the apparent contradiction between total love of God and self-love? If self-love or love of any other creature without this total reference to God is sin, then the sinless life of grace with God, the life of *agape*, charity, which is the essence of eternal salvation, is achieved only by a corresponding total lack of self-love in a total love of God. Is this possible?

We might at this point delve into some medieval texts which try to puzzle out this problem, but for purposes of interest and pertinence to our own times it will be more rewarding,

I think, to consider some answers to this problem under two illustrative groupings of later Lutheran and Catholic scholarship on the subject: *Agape and Eros*, by the Protestant Swedish bishop and scholar, Anders Nygren, and *The Mind and Heart of Love*, by the English Jesuit scholar, Martin D'Arcy, S.J.

3 THE LUTHERAN AND CATHOLIC TRADITIONS

Bishop Nygren devotes 680 pages of his 741-page work to developing the position that all theories of love, from the Greeks to the present and including those of the Catholic tradition in the Middle Ages, never really surpassed the essentially Greek idea of *eros*, the idea that man could regain his wholeness by his own effort, with God in the picture only partially or not at all. The medievals, of course, used the word *agape*, or charity, and developed doctrines about it; but Nygren contends that they always thought of this new *agape*, this fellowship with God which Christ proclaimed, as something to be achieved by self-help—a clear indication of its pagan content. Evidence of this, he says, would be the various programs, regimens, spiritual exercises, ascetic styles of life, etc., that one finds in use from the ancient Greeks to Plotinus and through the whole Christian tradition up to, but excluding, Martin Luther. Because of these concepts of self-effort in all of them, Nygren argues that their concept of Christian charity, love, was still essentially Greek in its conceptual content. Nygren lines up the contrasting notions of pagan and Christian love (understanding by Christian now Luther's conception of it) thus:

1 Eros is acquisitive desire and longing.	Agape is sacrificial giving.
2 Eros is an upward movement.	Agape comes down.
3 Eros is man's way to God.	Agape is God's way to man.
4 Eros is man's effort: it assumes that man's salvation is his own work.	Agape is God's grace: salvation is the work of divine love.

5 Eros is egocentric love, a form of self-assertion of the highest, noblest, sublimest kind.

Agape is unselfish love, it "seeketh not its own," it gives itself away.

6 Eros seeks to gain its life, a life divine, immortalized.

Agape lives the life of God, therefore dares to "lose it."

7 Eros is the will to get and possess, which depends on want and need.

Agape is freedom in giving, which depends on wealth and plenty.

8 Eros is primarily man's love; God is the object of Eros. Even when it is attributed to God, Eros is patterned on human love.

Agape is primarily God's love; God is Agape. Even when it is attributed to man, Agape is patterned on divine love.

9 Eros is determined by the quality, the beauty and worth, of its object; it is not spontaneous but "evoked," "motivated."

Agape is sovereign in relation to its object, and is directed to both "the evil and the good," it is spontaneous, "overflowing," "unmotivated."

10 Eros recognizes value in its object—and loves it.

Agape loves—and creates value in its object.[9]

It all comes down to saying that *agape* is "God's love," which comes to man with absolutely nothing of man entering into the reality of that *agape* that descends upon him. In other words, Nygren would answer the problem of disinterested love by saying that it is indeed possible, but that it is possible only if God gives a man the gift of *agape*, of loving God absolutely and without any motive of self-gain. No man can achieve *agape* in any way by his own efforts. And let us recall that *agape* here means the life of charity, of fellowship with God, which is the essential requisite for eternal salvation. On the plane of their own human efforts, men move in selfishness, in *eros*, in sin. But on the plane of faith, of redemption, *agape* is possible. This is precisely Christ's message, that it is God's will to come down to man.

Bishop Nygren believes that Luther and Luther alone caught this authentic note of *agape*, since Luther alone held the absolute nothingness of human effort vis-à-vis the descent of *agape* from God. Man can only believe, *"sola fides"*; God does the rest. If God gives you *agape*, you will love God disinterestedly; if not, nothing you can do will avail you of such a gift. From page 680 to the end of his book, Nygren talks of Luther's "Copernican revolution" that reversed all traditional conceptions of love and charity and showed that man can never hope to reach this new authenticity of love unless God gives it to him. "Luther's main objection to Catholic piety," says Nygren, "is always this: it puts man's own self in place of God."

Some sample texts from Luther may help at this point:

> . . . For God wills to save us not by domestic, but by extraneous righteousness and wisdom, not that which comes and springs from us, but that which comes from elsewhere into us, not that which originates in our earth, but that which comes down from heaven. Therefore, it behooves us to be instructed in a righteousness altogether external and alien. Wherefore it is first necessary that our own and domestic righteousness should be rooted out.[10]

This total helplessness of man before the face of God to achieve *agape*, which yet must be had for man to be saved, is characterized by Nygren as Luther's conception of "fellowship with God on the basis of sin, not of holiness." So again Luther can say:

> Thus monasteries and all religious under heaven are condemned; all cults are condemned inasmuch as they seek to furnish righteousness.[11]

As an Augustinian monk, Luther had read St. Bonaventure's *Itinerarium Mentis in Deum* and tried to live the ascetic practices recommended there. It was out of this background that he wrote of man's effort to achieve *agape* or union with God, who is Agape or Love, and the sheer futility of it all.

> I read Bonaventura on that subject, but he drove me nearly mad, because I wanted to experience the union of God with my soul (about which he talks nonsense) by the union of understanding and will. They are merely fanatical spirits.[12]

Nygren sees Luther as talking about love and at the same time *agape* in man, even though (as Luther points out) man is completely passive before God's unilateral initiation of Agape:

> At first sight, it might seem to be a depreciation of love, as if only faith, but not love, were excellent enough to find a place in the fundamental relationship to God. But such an idea is a complete misunderstanding of Luther's meaning. It is certainly not because love is not high and divine enough that Luther wishes to see it excluded from justification. If it only depended on its standing and excellence, Luther himself declares, he would be ready to set it alongside, nay, higher than, faith. Love is nothing other than God Himself, and therefore Luther can say of the man who abides in love, "that he and God become one cake ('*eine Kuche*')." Through faith we are children of God, but through love we are "gods," since to give in love is God's own nature.[13]

In Bishop Nygren's presentation, the Catholic tradition of the Middle Ages on the question of love is summarized under the rubric *fides caritate formata* ("faith infused with charity")—or more to the point, faith with good works. Again, all Catholic practices such as retreats, spiritual exercises, and ascetical regimens, etc., are looked upon critically as revelatory of their essentially pagan character, since ascent to union with God (the fullest form of the kind of love we are talking about) is seen in terms of self-effort, self-help. Nor is that self-help element merely a lingering, incidental residue in the whole process. Nygren analyzes the *fides caritate formata* tradition as essentially characterized by man's attempt to ascend from the human level to the divine level through his efforts, even though the ascent is explicitly predicated on the sole condition of God's gratuitously given grace of charity. Once *agape* is given, so Nygren understands the medieval tradition to have held, man then exerts his efforts at completing this life of grace by working, by striving to ascend into a unitive life of God. This to Nygren, who follows Luther on this point, is futile.[14]

To say that everyone before Luther looked on salvation as the work of *eros* is, in Nygren's understanding, equivalent to saying that they looked upon the carrying out of certain rules and regulations, certain programs—therefore LAW, in short—as the means of salvation. It is interesting to note in this connection that when Kant, himself a Protestant Pietist, puzzled out what the command to love meant, he came to the conclusion that it meant the acts or works of love, since it seemed clear to him that love in the emotional sense could not be commanded. In contrast to this position, Nygren presents Luther's interpretation of salvation as achieved on the basis of the GOSPEL, of authentic *agape*, where the only element to enter from the human side is a man's faith or belief. Luther describes the tremendous moment of illumination in his own life when he came to this conclusion:

> I was long in error and knew not how I was therein . . . till at last I came upon the place in *Rom. i*: "The righteous shall live by faith." That helped me. Then I saw of what righteousness Paul speaks: there stood in the text "righteousness"; then I put the abstract and concrete together and became sure of my case, learned to distinguish between the righteousness of the law and of the gospel. Before, I lacked nothing but that I made no distinction between law and gospel, and held them to be all one, and used to say that Christ differed not from Moses save in time and perfection. But when I found the distinction, that the law was one thing, the gospel another, then I broke through.[15]

In a paragraph that contrasts the medieval understanding of *agape*, or grace, to the "evangelical" viewpoint, Nygren summarizes the differences:

> In the Catholic manner, grace and fellowship with God are two different things: grace is the means, fellowship with God the end; in the Protestant manner, they coincide: grace is God's gracious will, in virtue of which He enters into fellowship with us sinners. In the former case, grace is a quality that is given to man; in the latter it is the good pleasure of God under which the man who is justified by God lives. In the former case, grace is the power which sets in motion man's upward-directed love, his Eros; in the latter case, it is the same as God's Agape.[16]

All this is the gist, at least, of Bishop Nygren's position that only Luther caught the authentic Christian message of *agape* as an absolute, one-sided descent of God into fellowship with sinful men, thereby saving them by his unilateral action.

Catholic dissent, predictably, was not long in coming, in the form of the Jesuit Martin D'Arcy's book, *The Mind and Heart of Love*. What bothered Father D'Arcy about Nygren's book was the cancellation of the human element in that interpretation of authentic love. If *agape* is totally one-sided, from God, how can it be in any way human at all? Luther answered this, as we have seen, by saying God and man become "one cake" when *agape* takes place. But this did not satisfy D'Arcy, who was concerned to preserve the classic Catholic teaching that grace does not destroy but rather builds on nature. *Agape*, or charity, should then only heighten and intensify authentic human love, not cancel it out of the picture altogether as Nygren's presentation seemed to do.

> Nygren thinks that all traces of self must be removed. In demanding this, he is asking the impossible. A love in which the self did not enter would be no love at all. The Christian always knows that God is not the kind of being who destroys what he has created out of love. Quite the opposite! He is the archetype of love, who always wishes well to his beloved.[17]

What then is human love, as D'Arcy sees it, on which grace builds in an agapeic context? Human love, he holds, like the universal rule of give-and-take in our changing universe, must contain both altruistic and self-centered elements if it is to be authentically human. Heart, feeling, sentiment, emotion, etc., in the lover are seen as literally ecstatic, projecting the lover beyond himself in an act of self-giving to the beloved. Mind, intellect, reason—as always, the specifying description of man's existential reality—is the limiting principle, reining man back in from irrational self-giving and making him work out the balance between his ecstatic tendencies and his self-interest. Human love is not all intellectual, as the Greeks tended to say when they tried to bare the essence of authentic human love. Yet neither is it all heart, precisely because the self-reflexive power of mind in man enables him to judge and evaluate the worthiness of his own self-giving. There is no question but that charity, or agapeic love, from God's side is gratuitous and free. But the question is how to merge human and divine love.

> Nygren cuts the knot and sunders self-love and grace, nature and the supernatural, completely. This does not make a peace between the two, but only a solitude in which Agape withers.[18]

To repeat, Father D'Arcy stresses the necessity of saving the dualistic aspect of authentic human love:

> If the self becomes entirely self-centered, a monstrous egoism follows, but as the self is now living on its own conceit and without external nourishment, the inflation is followed by collapse, a period of melancholia and death. If, following the opposite line, the self abandons itself to ecstatic love, it moves like a moth to the candle, or passively, like the musk rose, it gives forth a stronger perfume in the dark to entice the robber visitant of the night. It has chosen to be a victim, to die of love and to find its sole joy in self-immolation. . . . The two must never be separated.[19]

How this human love, combining both *eros* and *agape*, relates to the traditional command to contexture all human loves in the love of God, is worked out by D'Arcy in the final pages of his book. He does so in terms of the distinction between nature and person, and even more ultimately in terms of a metaphysics of existence that roots all beings and becomings in their Infinite Divine Source. Perhaps one can say that, basically, D'Arcy deepens and refines Aquinas' resolution of the problem of "disinterested love," and does so in terms of Aquinas' own metaphysical insight into "existence and essence." Aquinas' own answer, however, in terms of "part and whole" and "image and original" still form the base of Father D'Arcy's reconciliation of human love, with its erotic and agapeic aspects, with the love of God. But what is this "part and whole," "image and original" theory of Aquinas?

I think it best, perhaps, to give Etienne Gilson's classic description of the theory. Before Gilson, in a book called *Problème de L'Amour*, a French Dominican, Pierre Rousselot, had researched the problem in Aquinas and had demonstrated textually that Aquinas resolved the problem of disinterested love in terms of part and whole, a position that came to be known as the physicalist solution to the problem.[20] Briefly, it maintained that there is no conflict between human loves and divine love, since in loving God (the Whole) man can and does love each of his particular loves within that whole. Even as the hand instinctively goes up to ward off a blow, thereby illustrating the presence in a single action of both self-centered and altruistic elements, so in one act man can encompass both human and divine love. Obviously, in sacrificing itself so the man may live on, the hand is altruistic. But it is also self-centered, at least insofar as without the hand's interposition the blow would kill the man, and so the hand would surely go out of existence. It is a rich insight. Translated to other situations, this insight would mean that the father of a family, for example, could really love his family altruistically and "selfishly" at once and without conflict. For it is the whole family he loves, and since he is genuinely united to them in love, life would be nothing to him without them. Therefore, in expending himself altruistically for them, he is at the same time looking out for his own self-interest.

Gilson, however, is not happy with this presentation from Aquinas. His own position, likewise supported by texts in Aquinas, is that of image and original. His critique of the part and whole resolution, as well as his own position on image and original is as follows:

> There is some truth in this interpretation of the Thomist doctrine of love, but this something is exposed to falsification by something else that is not true at all. The hand is really and literally a part of the body; and in this case it is quite true to say that the relation of the particular to the general good is the relation of a part to a whole. But

> as soon as we leave this biological example . . . we can no longer
> hold the same formula. . . . It is still true to say that God is the uni-
> versal Good under which all particular goods are contained, but the
> relation of dependence in which man stands to God is no longer that
> of a part to its Whole . . . it differs even from the rational process
> which prompts the citizen to sacrifice himself for the City.[21]

He thinks his own theory of image and original is really more
consistent with the Thomistic theories of participation and
analogy of being.

> If we say that each good is but a particular good, we can only mean
> not that these particular goods are detached parts of a whole which
> would be Goodness, but that they are analogues of the creative Good
> that gave them birth. In this sense, then, it is true that to love any
> good whatsoever is always to love its resemblance to the divine good-
> ness, and, since it is this resemblance to God that makes this good to
> be a good, we can say that what is loved in it is the Sovereign Good.
> In other words, it is impossible to love the image without at the
> same time loving the original, and if we know, as we do know, that
> the image is only an image, it is impossible to love it without prefer-
> ring the original. To will any object is to will an image of God, that
> is, to will God; to love oneself, then, will be to love an analogue of
> God, and that is to love God.[22]

We can go back now and see how Father D'Arcy's own
presentation goes beyond the "part and whole" theory of
Rousselot, and the "image and original" theory of Gilson, to the
dialectic of essence and existence. To D'Arcy's mind, man, as
specified by his rational intellect, shows precisely what kind of
existence is his. And since the role of understanding or intellect
is one of assimilation, of a taking in of the world and of its own
self into itself, D'Arcy understands this to be the masculine
aspect of human love, *animus*, that which looks out for the subject's own self-interest. The human will, as the human faculty
for loving, D'Arcy characterizes as outgoing, ecstatic, the femi-
nine aspect of human love, *anima*. Left to itself, *anima* tends
to give of itself totally and without due regard of self, in an
irrational form of self-immolation. The harmonious balance of

the two therefore is what constitutes for D'Arcy the authenticity of human love: *animus* and *anima*, giving and taking in a fine balance and unity, just as the one human being is composed metaphysically of essence (human) and existence (being).

Father D'Arcy, therefore, tries to reach the higher synthesis of human and divine love through *existence*. Following what is now known among Thomists as the formalistic interpretation of St. Thomas' doctrine of being,[23] D'Arcy makes such statements as these: "It will be remembered that existence adds nothing to the essence save to make it actual."[24] "On the other hand, existence is for the sake of the essence, and in this respect essence is superior to existence."[25] "Existence gives nothing to the essence; it only actualizes it."[26] Such language all too easily gives the impression of interpreting *esse*, the act of being, as receiving something from essence other than limitation; in that respect, many interpreters of Aquinas today would deny that this is Aquinas' teaching.

Be that as it may, D'Arcy does say in a number of places that essence is indeed the limiting, receiving principle of existence, and that existence by itself would be unlimited—indeed, that existence is the root of the centrifugal, disinterested direction of love in man. Existence, itself unlimited as the perfecting principle and limited only by the receiving principle of essence, tends beyond any limits toward its own fullness. This is the first way in which the springs of disinterested love are built in man and made concrete in the power of willing, or of loving, which, unlike the intellect, tends toward things just as they exist, not as they are received in the intellect. The will, in loving, goes out toward other existences.

There is also a second way in which the presence of disinterested love may be understood as present in man. His existence is precisely a caused existence, one ultimately received from the fullness of Existence, i.e., God. There is therefore a constant correlation or correspondence between the caused existence in man and God who causes that existence. And finite human existence, in tending toward other existences, other human beings, etc., ultimately tends toward its divine source. So D'Arcy no longer uses the imagery of part and whole, or image and original, but that of "syntonization," which he explains in this way:

> It is as if the sounding of a note on one instrument produced the corresponding note on another instrument, or as if a child were to begin to hum and dance as it listened to a fiddler playing outside the window. The energy of love, which is God's own, is communicated, and an essentially inferior energy starts repeating the rhythm of the superior one in its fashion, as when a log thrown into a stream takes on the motion of the stream or a rider on horseback sways up and down to the movement of the horse. Causality is a kind of *pas de deux*, the sympathetic response in a finite being energizing to the simple, supreme energizing of the Creator. The conductor, who is also the composer, lifts his baton and each member plays and gives back to him his own music.[27]

If one scrutinizes D'Arcy for reasons why this twofold human love still needs divine union and how, supposedly in contrast to Nygren's position, D'Arcy's account of united human and divine love preserves the human, one is not at all sure that D'Arcy makes the point convincingly:

> As in his essential movement a human being turns within, in his existential movement he turns without—and if we ask the ultimate reason why there should be such diverse movements within the one self, the answer is that it is limited, that the essence of the finite self is not its existence, and that only in God do the two loves unite. God is what he is, and hence the centripetal love is a movement between persons who are one in essence.[28]

Yet D'Arcy keeps insisting:

> . . . in the Christian Agape the complete revelation of love is given. Here the finite is not left to itself to repeat in the perfection of its nature the divine beauty and to crave to belong to God. The finite is lifted to a new degree of being, whose limit is measured only by the necessity of its remaining a human person. This new energizing has for its object to change the relation of creature to creator into one of friend with friend, beloved and loved. This new life which is

thus set going is a pure gift and beyond the natural capacity of the finite human person; the self has the joy of knowing that it is now so united to the life of God that even the beginning of its own acts and love is God's. It now lives in me. It expresses the perfection of personal relations; all is giving and there is no thought of taking; what one has is the gift of the other.[29]

Father D'Arcy thus holds that the twofold aspect of human love, of give and take, of heart and mind, is totally synthesized with divine love, even as it remains its finite self in that union. Why? Because man's self is an intellectual one, and thus is always able to recognize its own state of union. The last words in his book remind the reader of Nygren's error:

In this *agape* all that Nygren demanded is present. God is all in all, and there is no trace of that kind of self-love which interferes with perfect love. But self is there, and self and the intellect, for it is God who loves them and gives them both increase.[30]

To conclude this debate, however, let me quote what Bishop Nygren wrote in subsequent editions of his book after reading Father D'Arcy's work:

In the discussion of the subject that has so far taken place, I have found no reason to abandon my original position at any point, and my work is therefore being republished without alteration.[31]

One need not side either way in this debate to appreciate how large a role faith played in the medieval consciousness. As St. Bonaventure and St. Bernard used to say, if a man just went by reason, how could he ever come to the saving mysteries of redemption? How could a man live like Christ, as Christians are called to, if one went by reason alone? For reason, as we saw in D'Arcy, is always self-concerned. How could reason begin to comprehend the "emptying" of God at every turn in the mysteries of creation, incarnation, crucifixion, etc.? That there have been innumerable instances in the Catholic tradition of excesses on the part of lovers and followers of Christ becomes a bit more understandable when, like St. Paul, we realize that for them "to live is Christ."

On the day-to-day level, too, one need not live so very long to see how human relations feed on interpersonal faith, beyond what is purely rational, when they endure and grow. What would happen if, in the wholing process of love, husband and wife related to one another on the purely balanced, natural way of give-and-take Father D'Arcy describes? Are we not often faced with the "absurd" in the other, which we yet take on faith to be for the better—and it does turn out for the better in terms of the wholing process deepening and enriching itself? Perhaps the role of *agape*, to one who believes, is precisely to confirm and elevate this natural faith demanded of every one who strives for wholeness.

Beyond the context of the medieval debate on love, though, we may profitably look now at the idea of love as wholing in two other Christian thinkers who struggled with the meaning-of-life question, Søren Kierkegaard and Dietrich Bonhoeffer.

4 RECENT CHRISTIAN IDEAS OF LOVE

A *Søren Kierkegaard* (1813-1855)

Let us bypass many of Søren Kierkegaard's phrases now in popular use and go straight to our issue by considering his notion of faith: an affirmation of God and his infinite being in the teeth of the absurd, that is, in the face not only of uncertain but even downright opposing evidence about God's existence in the objective world. Kierkegaard mocked philosophers who expended effort in proving God's existence. For objectively, according to Kierkegaard, in the world around us there are more than enough signs against that existence. God has absolutely nothing obvious about him. He is invisible. It is that simple. Subjectively, for the one trying to prove God's existence, there already exists within him the "ideal interpretation" which enables the prover to recognize his premises, whatever they may be, precisely as signs *of God*.[32]

But how does one arrive at that "ideal interpretation," since it is not gotten by proofs? It can come only through the subjective faith of the inward man, who shows himself in dialectical opposition to objective uncertainty. Needless to say, this hardly comes without an internal turmoil of fear and trembling, resignation, sickness almost to despair, all of which are mastered through the "infinite passion" of faith, faith pure and of a single eye:

> Without risk there is no faith. Faith is precisely the contradiction between the infinite passion of the individual awareness and the objective uncertainty. If I am capable of grasping God objectively, I do not believe; but precisely because I cannot do this, I must believe. If I wish to preserve myself in faith, I must constantly be intent upon the deep, over seventy thousand fathoms of water, still preserving my faith.[33]

Without this inward affirmation of the infinite, maturing in man to the point of radical transformation, a man does not refind, "repeat" himself. But with this inward affirmation of God, specifically of Christ, man, in leaving all the rest behind him, paradoxically repossesses all, including self, in this new relationship with God.

We need not recall the details of Kierkegaard's own personal life, how from his childhood onward he turned his attention toward God and infinity. "The dialectic of faith is the finest and most remarkable of all. I am able to make from this springboard the great leap whereby I pass into infinity."[34] Our precise interest in all this dialectical structure of faith is not so much on the subject-object level (man-world) as it is in the final leap of the individual to God, alone to the Alone. Because of the presence of the "ideal interpretation" in man, who through inwardness affirms that ideal interpretation, it appears that the leap is not made from absolute nothingness on the side of man to everything in God. For what is Kierkegaard's idea of the man who leaps into this "repetition" of himself in God? If he rediscovers his own self in God, it is fair to surmise that he somehow already had the beginnings of that self before the leap. What then is this man?

> Man is a spirit. But what is spirit? Spirit is the self. But what is the self? The self is a relation which relates itself to its ownself, or it is that in the relation that the relation relates itself to its own self; the self is not the relation but consists in the fact that the relation relates itself to its own self. Man is a synthesis of the infinite and the finite, of the temporal and the eternal, of freedom and necessity; in short this is a synthesis. A synthesis is a relation between two factors. So regarded, man is not yet a self.[35]

This sort of language could easily make a reader despair. Yet it makes sense when one recalls how Kierkegaard likened the act of faith in God to a man drowning in the deep sea, who, at the very moment of letting go, of resigning everything he has in the world, repossesses them anew in God. The passage above talks of infinity present within the self, "a relation which relates itself to its ownself," which infinity the self then affirms. This is done through the great act of faith in which the self moves itself to its new relationship with its own ground of being. Twice Kierkegaard states:

> This then is the formula which describes the condition of the self when despair is completely eradicated: by the relating itself to its own self and by willing to be itself, the self is grounded transparently in the Power which posited it.[36]

As a man moves through the various spheres of aesthetic, ethical, and religious existence, he already bears within himself the eternal, waiting to be affirmed through faith in order to pass into wholeness with God, specifically with Christ.

> The potentiation in consciousness of the self is in this instance knowledge of Christ, being a self face to face with Christ. First there came ignorance of having an eternal self; then knowledge of having a self wherein there is after all something eternal; then a self which has a human conception of itself or whose goal is man. The contrast to this was a self face to face with God. The more conception of Christ, the more self.[37]

We see here the passage of a man progressively growing toward what Kierkegaard considers the authentic self, as a man measures himself and looks toward higher and higher relation-

ships as processive goals. These goals in turn show a certain
pattern, a tearing away of the individual from everything else
and a movement toward God alone, who then makes possible
the refinding of everything that was lost before the self's birth
in repetition.

> Despair is potentiated in proportion to consciousness of self, but the
> self is potentiated in the ratio of the measure proposed for the self,
> and infinitely potentiated when God is the measure. The more con-
> ception of God, the more self; the more self, the more conception of
> God. Only when the self as this definite individual is conscious of
> existing before God, only then is it the infinite self.[38]

Finally we may note that, true to the Protestant Lutheran
conception of faith we saw in Nygren, Kierkegaard also identifies the act of faith itself with God's saving grace. And this is
love, the highest love, charity. "A believer is surely a lover,
yea, of all lovers the most in love."[39] From this supernatural
vantage point we see the equation of self and conscience, of
being and becoming, in a whole-making relationship between
the individual and God:

> Love is a matter of conscience, and hence is not a matter of impulse
> and inclination; nor is it a matter of emotion, nor a matter for intel-
> lectual calculation.[40]

So Kierkegaard writes of the self, at its highest point of standing before God in all purity of heart: "Love believes everything, and is never deceived." For it is one and the same thing
for the self to believe everything and to love unconditionally.
And it is clear what for Kierkegaard is the One Unconditional
Good that is worth one's unconditional love.

We may also remark in passing that these tortured passages
on man finding his true self in God were born of Kierkegaard's
own tragic life, made all the more painful by his sensitive temperament. He suffered, and searched his sufferings for whatever lonely meaning they would yield him. But this is clearly
beyond our present scope.

B *Dietrich Bonhoeffer* (1906-1945)

It is sometimes customary to explain the shift from the Old Testament to the New by pointing to the earthly sanctions God meted out in the former and the spiritual ones emphasized in the latter. Dietrich Bonhoeffer's key insight for the purpose of our discussion may be seen in a passage which rejects this view, a view Bonhoeffer saw as outdated but which Kierkegaard followed. There are passages in the New Testament, Bonhoeffer says, that still affirm God's encounter with man in immediate environmental contexts. And it is this agonizing search for God as the meaning of life not in any remote sense but in the immediacy of life, or even of fate itself, that endears Bonhoeffer to any reader who, though Christian, like Bonhoeffer, is undergoing the painful process of searching out life's meaning.

> Now, is it an accident that sickness and death are mentioned in connection with the misuse of the Lord's supper? Is it right to set the Old Testament blessing against the cross? This is what Kierkegaard did. That makes the cross, or at least suffering, an abstract principle and that is just what gives rise to an unhealthy methodism which deprives suffering of its element of contingency on a divine ordinance.[41]

Discernment of God's will and work experientially and in the immediacy of one's environment, as against the old style of belief that knew it all from a book or had it all written out and memorized beforehand, is Dietrich Bonhoeffer's concern. Suffering was certainly no abstract thing for him; he wrote in a Nazi concentration camp. Yet we find him never faltering in his faith in God, though ever struggling to relate God as the meaning of his life to his own concrete circumstances in prison. Bonhoeffer considered this matter of knowing beforehand what God's will is for man collectively and for each man individually, no matter what the circumstances of life, a *deus ex machina* no longer suitable for a technological world "come of age." Many of the things and events men previously prayed and petitioned to God for are now within man's own power to produce. And it is in this world in which God is the "beyond in our midst" that the meaning of life, even for a believer, is to be found.

> God would have us know that we must live as men who manage our lives without him. The God who is with us is the God who forsakes us (Mark 15:34). The God who lets us live in the world without the working hypothesis of God is the God before whom we stand continually. Before God and with God we live without God. Here is the decisive difference between Christianity and all religions. Man's religiosity makes him look in his distress to the power of God in the world: God is thus *deus ex machina*. The Bible directs man to God's powerlessness and suffering: only the suffering God can help. To that extent we may say that the development towards the world's coming of age outlined above, which has done away with a false conception of God, opens up a way of seeing the God of the Bible who wins power and space in the world by his weakness.[42]

One can sense here Bonhoeffer's obsession to concentrate on man, his fellowmen, right at the time and place of their sufferings, and to identify the meaning of life, God, Christ, faith, and the self—all these—in one's service for others, in being a "man for others." Any other type of faith that makes the slightest separation of God from the concrete circumstances of life was unacceptable to Bonhoeffer:

> The transcendental is not infinite and unattainable tasks, but the neighbor who is within reach in any given situation.[43]

> I discovered later, and I am still discovering right up to this moment, that it is only by living completely in this world that one learns to have faith. One must completely abandon any attempt to make something of oneself, whether it be a saint, or a converted sinner, or a churchman (a so-called priestly type!), a righteous man or an unrighteous one, a sick man or a healthy one. By this-worldliness I mean living unreservedly in life's duties, problems, successes and failures, experiences and perplexities. In so doing we throw ourselves completely into the arms of God, taking seriously not our own sufferings, but those of God in the world, watching with Christ in Gethsemane. That I think is faith, that is metanoia; and that is how one becomes a man and a Christian.[44]

But just how concretely does Christ and the meaning of one's life coincide at the point of experience?

> The experience of a transformation of all human life is given in the fact that "Jesus is there only for others." His "being there for others" is the experience of transcendence. It is only this "being for others," maintained till death, that is the ground of his omnipotence, omniscience, and omnipresence. Faith is participation in this being, Jesus (incarnation, cross, and resurrection).[45]

If one goes on to ask what is this man we should serve as Christians, he finds Bonhoeffer sometimes talking of man as a whole man, but also and emphatically of man as not-yet whole, of man awaiting wholeness through Christ. In one sense, of course, man is whole—and it is fallacious to split him into internal and external selves, as when we say of someone "He is really good inside, though just looking at him from the outside you wouldn't think so." But we find the two aspects of man as both whole and yet still awaiting wholeness explained in Bonhoeffer thus:

> . . . it is thought that a man's essential nature consists of his inmost and most intimate background; that is defined as his "inner life" and it is precisely in those secret human places that God is to have his domain! . . . The Bible does not recognize our distinction between the outward and the inward. Why should it? It is always concerned with *anthropos teleios*, the whole man. "The heart" in the Biblical sense is not the inner life, but the whole man in relation to God. But as a man lives just as much from "outwards" to "inwards" as from "inwards" to "outwards," the view that his essential nature can be understood only from his intimate spiritual background is wholly erroneous.[46]

Our relations to other men shape and mold our internal attitudes as much as our internal thoughts and attitudes shape our relations to other men, and God is to be found in the totality and concreteness of those relations. His will, too, can be discerned in those concrete relations. Hence, for Dietrich Bonhoeffer the *ought* (God's will) and the *is* (the concrete circumstances in which the divine will is embedded) are united just as they were once united in a manifest way in God before the fall.

For Bonhoeffer, then, the wholeness of man can finally be found in life in Christ through faith. Before this, everything else is less than final, is *penultimate*, and cannot regain the original wholeness lost through the fall.[47] Our own life situation, he says,

> . . . makes us particularly aware of the fragmentary and incomplete nature of our own. But this very fragmentariness may, in fact, point towards a fulfillment beyond the limits of human achievement; I have to keep that in mind, particularly in view of the death of so many of the best of my former pupils. Even if the pressure of outward events may split our lives into fragments, like bombs falling on houses, we must do our best to keep in view how the whole was planned and thought out.[48]

There is no ascesis or method then, thinks Bonhoeffer, by which man recovers his original wholeness, except the very general one of faith in Christ. This general faith, however, is substantialized only in the concrete decision to be a man for others, which itself falls short of the "whole man" until it is related to the wholeness of Christ.

> In these turbulent times we repeatedly lose sight of what really makes life worth living. We think that, because this or that person is living, it makes sense for us to live too. But the truth is that this earth was good enough for the man Jesus Christ, that such a man as Jesus lived; then, and only then has life meaning for us. If Jesus had not lived then our lives would be meaningless, in spite of all the other people whom we know and honor and love. The unbiblical idea of "meaning" is indeed only a translation of what the Bible calls "promise."[49]

To the end, we find Dietrich Bonhoeffer ever the heroic Christian, struggling with the meaning-of-life problem in seeking out Christ in the concrete circumstances of life which all too often, in this technological age, obscured that vision. How to get "guidance" out of "fate" (*schicksal*) was the tormented way he expressed his search for wholeness.

LOVE, DEATH, AND BEYOND

From positions which adhere to God and Christ in every-thing that concerns the wholing of the individual, the fragment, we now move again dialectically to the position of Freud and the neo-Freudians who reject the divine and spiritual dimen-sions in man altogether. Here we shall find the concept of wholing confined solely to a bodily context. For balance, we will then go to some notions of love as a wholing process that thrusts precisely toward the spiritual, though always with the body as the supporting force of that thrust. And in treating this latter position we will discuss the thoughts of Gabriel Marcel and Jules Toner, S.J.

1 FREUD AND NEO-FREUDIANS

No man can live for any considerable length of time with-out coming up against a problematic situation. By problematic situation in this context is meant a moment of instability, an unbalancing of the organism, something that usually pains the organism. This painful tension, in turn, naturally causes the or-ganism to seek to restore the pleasurable state of equilibrium it enjoyed before the moment of problematic tension.[1] If one is successful in achieving a new equilibrium, either mentally by finding a satisfactory answer to a tormenting question, or physically by assimilating the new elements that gave rise to the problem, a synthesis richer than the organism's previous state or condition results.

And so, in Freud's thought, *eros*, the pleasure principle, moves ever onward toward richer and richer syntheses through new modes of equilibrium: *ungebändigt immer vorwärts dringt* ("it presses ever forward unsubdued").[2] It is interesting that when Freud tried to puzzle out this human phenomenon of *eros* striving incessantly for equilibrium, he found no plausible scientific explanation but only a philosophical one which, as Freud himself notes, went back to the Aristophanic myth in the *Symposium*[3] about which he writes in *Beyond the Pleasure Principle*:

> I should not venture to produce it were it not that it fulfills precisely the one condition whose fulfillment we desire. For it traces the origin of an instinct to a need to restore an earlier state of things. What I have in mind, of course, is the theory which Plato put into the mouth of Aristophanes in the *Symposium*, and which deals not only with the origin of the sexual instinct, but also with the most important of its variations in relation to its object.[4]

Freud then develops his idea of how *eros*, or the pleasure principle, proceeds from equilibrium to equilibrium through new states of tension:

> Shall we follow the hint given us by the poet-philosopher, and venture upon the hypothesis that living substance at the time of its coming to life was torn apart into small particles, which have ever since endeavored to reunite through the sexual instincts? That these instincts, in which the chemical affinity of inanimate matter persisted, gradually succeeded, as they developed through the kingdom of protista, in overcoming the difficulties put in the way of that endeavor by an environment charged with dangerous stimuli—stimuli which compelled them to form a protective cortical layer? That these splintered fragments of living substance in this way attained a multicellular condition and finally transferred the instinct for reuniting, in the most highly concentrated form, to the germ cells?[5]

Here we meet the peculiar vein in Freud's thought that all our steps forward are really steps backwards! What we really do when we go from rich synthesis to richer synthesis, and so on and on, is to move paradoxically toward the absolute equilibrium we once possessed when we were one whole with the cosmos, before the bombarding stimuli forced the first protrusion of life from the cosmic surface. This "compulsion to repeat" what happened in the universe at large is found in every individual. Ontogenesis recapitulates phylogenesis; that is to say, the history of all life motions in the cosmos is reenacted in the life of every individual man.

> The attributes of life were at some time evoked in inanimate matter by the action of a force of whose nature we can form no conception. It may perhaps have been a process similar in type to that which later caused the development of consciousness in a particular stratum of living matter. The tension which then arose in what had hitherto been an inanimate substance endeavored to cancel itself out. In this way the first instinct came into being: the instinct to return to the inanimate state.[6]

In this Freudian theme, *eros* and *thanatos* ("love" and "death") appear as two sides of one movement, conjugated to each other, or at any rate (if one disputes such a reduction of all instincts in Freud to one) surely co-related.[7] The movement forward toward richer equilibrium and synthesis is really one of easing tension, and thus what we really seek, because we subconsciously remember it, is the unity and harmony we once had, and which, with the first protrusion of life from the surface of the cosmos, we lost.

> If we take it as a truth that knows no exception that everything living dies for *internal* reasons—becomes inorganic once again—then we shall be compelled to say that the "aim of all life is death" and, looking backwards, that "inanimate things existed before living ones."[8]

We also find a variation of this motion toward the absolute equilibrium of death in Freud's notion of "polymorphous perverse sexuality." According to this conception, there was a time in our infancy (before the sixth year, said Freud)[9] when psychic wish and reality were one, when everything we ever desired was there for our enjoyment. The process of maturation, unfortunately, splinters us off from this childhood heaven, as we begin to discover that often we not only have to postpone gratification (the Freudian concept of maturity)[10] but forego gratification altogether. We learn to be realistic, to look around us and make adjustments in our performances (ego), since we see that total gratification of all our desires (id) is impossible. We work out, in other words, a system of repression, as love and work slowly predominate as the main preoccupations of our lives. Moreover, since in actuality a man can neither work nor love without some sort of repression, it is understandable that in our off moments we dream and fantasy situations where we can enjoy love's pleasures totally and without repression. Ultimately, even work itself is a form of repression for the sake of our love life.

Today, Herbert Marcuse maintains that Freud himself would probably modify his statement on the eternal necessity of repression if he were still around, since he would see that our scientific technology, if used wisely, would enable human communities to live under the twin stars of leisure and abundance. Every man would then be able to "do his own thing," achieving the age-old dream of man in which love and work are synonymous and man would be doing what he liked, thereby overcoming any interruption in his line of pleasure.

It was the thesis of *Eros and Civilization*, more fully developed in my *One Dimensional Man*, that man could avoid the fate of a Welfare through Warfare state only by achieving a new starting point where he could reconstruct the productive apparatus without that "innerworldly asceticism" which provided the basis for domination and exploration. This image of man was the determinate negation of Nietzsche's superman: man intelligent enough and healthy enough to dispense with all heroes and heroic virtues, man without the impulse to live dangerously, to meet the challenge; man with the good conscience to make life an end-in-itself, to live in joy a life without fear. "Polymorphous sexuality" was the term I used to indicate that a new direction of progress would depend completely on the opportunity to activate repressed or arrested organic, biological needs: to make the human body an instrument of pleasure rather than labor.[11]

In other words, we need to surpass Freud's position that the eternal, primordial struggle for existence which takes the form of work necessarily accompanies civilization.[12] Scientific technology today moves us out of the necessity of scarcity and want to the possibility of abundance and leisure, where every man would do just exactly what he enjoyed doing. And this fits into Philip Rieff's concept of contemporary man as "psychological man" or the "therapeutic," as detailed in his book *The Triumph of the Therapeutic*.

The "therapeutic" is not out to be a hero in a struggle for existence. In the past, this struggle often took the form of joining larger groups for security and protection, of making religious and organizational commitments, of performing feats of outstanding loyalty to that group. As Rieff sees it, the man emerging from today's cultural turmoils will move away from external commitments (from the challenges and heroic virtues demanded of Nietzschean man) toward the self as the center, the self's enjoyment of life itself as the goal of all living, a goal impossible before the era of our contemporary abundance. Previously, in the context of want, repression loomed large in the very idea of civilization. The new context will bring forth Nietzsche's idea of "the child in every man that wants to play."[13] And the base for all this, once again, is material abundance and proper modes of distribution. With the "primordial struggle for existence" overcome, there will be universal permissiveness for everyone to do "his own thing."

> Our cultural revolution does not aim, like its predecessor, at victory for some rival commitment, but rather at a way of using all commitments, which amounts to loyalty towards none. . . . Men will have ceased to seek any salvation other than the amplitude of life itself.[14]

Of course, there will always be interpersonal relationships and the consequent cross-fertilization of ideas, but this will not be, as in the past context of scarcity, relations of threat and impending rivalry, but rather of universal acceptance even of apparently incompatible beliefs, an ideal form of maturity.

> A tolerance of ambiguities is the key to what Freud considered the most difficult of all personal accomplishments: a genuinely stable character in an unstable time. . . . Indeed the therapy of all therapies, the secret of all secrets, the interpretation of all interpretations, in Freud, is not to attach oneself exclusively or too passionately to any one particular meaning or object.[15]

Even the churches of tomorrow will share this radical change from exclusive commitments to universal tolerance and celebration of an abundant life. A church then

> . . . will be a place of abandoned righteousness, of color, movement, and vitality where young and old will not only look at what men of past ages have painted, listen to what they have written and the music they have made, but where they themselves will be free to paint, dance, talk and express themselves in ways no longer easy in an age of automation, non-employment, space sickness, and leisure lostness.[16]

Even if one were to admit that it is not at all easy to discern what one really wants to be in life, since often it is the conflicts themselves that serve to reveal our deepest desires even to ourselves, one still has to reflect seriously on the ideas propounded here of moving away from unending multiplication of artificial needs and goods in a society conditioned by advertising to be happy whenever they can afford to purchase those goods, and turning instead toward genuine bodily satisfaction, a real earthly heaven of "polymorphous sexuality," as something within our reach today.[17]

In his book *Life Against Death*, Norman Brown uses this new context of fulfillment to interpret the traditional Christian belief of resurrection of the body. That resurrection, he thinks, should be understood in the light of Christ's injunction: "unless you become as little children, you shall not enter into the kingdom of heaven." This idea of equating heaven with a time in our infancy, when wish coincided with reality, is common among Freudians. Brown marshals his presentation of Freud toward one point: the coincidence of a man's life at its peak moment of fullness and fulfillment with death itself. We see here Brown's further development of Freud's combination of *eros-thanatos*; following the poet R. M. Rilke, Brown presents an interesting interpretation of the horror of death felt by every man. It is not so much horror simply at the thought of death, but rather of a premature or untimely death, of dying with "unlived lines in our bodies." Since everything perfect in nature spontaneously turns toward death, the perfect, resurrected body which the Christian creed promises would itself also wish to die![18]

One recalls that Brown's interpretation of the horror of death as horror of *premature* death is supported by the ancient Church's prayer in its Litany of the Saints for deliverance not from death simply, but precisely from a "sudden and unprovided death." One also recalls the story of how the famed heart-surgeon Christiaan Barnard, as a young man, came to this same insight and thereby decided to go on with his study of medicine. Death for any medical doctor is *the* enemy to be confronted and defeated, and yet as a young medical student Barnard not only fainted at the first sight of blood during an appendectomy, but he found it almost impossible to walk into a roomful of cadavers to practice dissection! He records his meditation in a little chapel in the same Groote Schuur Hospital where years later he was to perform the historical first heart transplant:

> Gradually, I came to see that what I had was not an isolated fear of death itself. My anguish and rage and yes, my fright, stemmed from premature death, by disease or error, the loss of life before it had run its span. Death was to be feared and treated as an enemy, depending on when it came. At the right hour, it was no longer to be

held back, indeed it was welcome. Father into your hands I commit my spirit.[19]

It may be good, too, to recall Nicolai Berdyaev's (1874-1948) remark that it is the realization that there is a termination point to one's life which enables a man to make it meaningful.[20] The very thought that our lives could at anytime end prematurely, and will at any rate certainly end, gives a certain tang and intensity to the wholing process we are engaged in. We savor our living moments all that much more with death in the background. The slackening in life's processes, and indeed the longing for death itself when it is taken out of the picture, is well expressed in the myth of Tithonus, who asked for immortality but forgot to ask along with it the corresponding gift of youth. Tennyson tries to capture the thoughts of Tithonus' aging self thus:

> The woods decay, the woods decay and fall,
> The vapours weep their burthen to the ground.
> Man comes and tills the field and lies beneath,
> And after many a summer dies the swan.
> Me only cruel immortality
> Consumes; I wither slowly in thine arms,
> Here at the quiet limit of the world,
> A white-haired shadow roaming like a dream
> The ever silent spaces of the East,
> Far-folded mists, and gleaming halls of morn.[21]

But to come back to Brown: he correctly interprets Karl Marx (1818-1883) as holding that, through exploitation of labor, the laborer has been alienated from his own powers. The new system hopefully dawning upon us seeks the recovery and enjoyment of all those powers, the "appropriation of the expropriated." (Our point here is not to controvert the many sides to this position, but simply to point up the worthiness of intensifying all human efforts toward eliminating premature death and enabling every man to be himself in a genuine enjoyment of life in this new age when a trip to the moon has become ordinary.) But the sticking point is ever present in Brown's thought: our view of all reality must not transcend the body.

> In the words of Thoreau: "We need pray for no higher heaven than the pure senses can furnish, a purely sensuous life. Our present senses are but rudiments of what they are destined to become!" The human body would become polymorphously perverse, delighting in that full life of all the body which it now fears. The consciousness strong enough to endure full life would be no longer Apollonian but Dionysian—consciousness which does not observe the limit but overflows; consciousness which does *not negate any more*.[22]

This then is one view of the wholing process open to a man who disavows anything of God and immortality and the whole story of Christian Redemption which, as we saw, were the central themes of medieval thought. We should now press our dialectical reflection further and trace out the thoughts of a contemporary existentialist philosopher who is similarly obsessed by the tendency to rivet every reflection deep within human experience and the human flesh, and yet somehow argues for a human reality that transcends death and the body as man strains in life to go from the self as a fragment to wholeness with others. We meet here the principal theme of Gabriel Marcel: *esse est coesse*, to be is to be with others.

2 GABRIEL MARCEL (1889—)

The kind of analysis Freud employs, in Marcel's view, voids reality of any significant value.[23] Indeed for Freud there are no intrinsic values inscribed in the universe, eternal salvation is a "great lie," and religion is merely a result of man's inability to accept his own insignificance in the universe. Since obviously Marcel's disagreement with these positions stems from his view of reality, it will help at this point to state that view briefly.

Marcel distinguishes reality into either the plane of existence or the plane of *being*. The plane of existence is that of mere objects, things which, in a way, are all surface without depth. Man is born into the midst of things, interacting with them on the level of existents, especially when he relates to them in a purely functional, utilitarian way and expends his life in efforts to *have* things. We have already remarked in our first chapter how there is a necessary coinciding between *to have* and *to be*, but this is not the point here. Rather, the stress is on contemporary technological man's proneness to universalize his attitude of *having*, even to the level of human relationships, and so to view persons in merely functional ways rather than as very privileged and valuable points of access to reality at its deepest, to *being*. Something there is in the human person that escapes all analysis: the deepest core of the person's reality, which is what one would have to enter to come to the realm of *being*.

> Being is what withstands—or what would withstand—an exhaustive analysis bearing on the data of experience and aiming to reduce them step by step to elements increasingly devoid of intrinsic or significant value. An analysis of this kind is attempted in the theoretical works of Freud.[24]

Any attempt to penetrate the personal core of being from the outside as though it were a scientific problem is doomed to failure, for the simple reason that man is not merely one more object in the universe and therefore should not be dealt with as such. Man is a subject; he is at the center of that which he questions and seeks to explore; he is a mystery, not a problem. Accordingly, one must go beyond objective analysis, no matter how disguised this may be by the rubric of interpreting symbols, to what Marcel calls "secondary reflection," a process of recapturing that which is revealed within me beyond the scientific, problematical procedure.

In secondary reflection, one perceives an emptiness within himself that cries out to be filled: an ontological *exigence-to-be*, the need to be. One thus sees oneself merely as a fragment desperately desiring completion, fullness. Yet, strangely, it is also within my power at this very point to turn away and absolutize myself, to make myself the center of all reality, thereby intensifying my own state of fragmentation. Beyond technical functions, and the having or being had by things and people, a person knows by some sort of "blind intuition" that his fragmentation is not necessarily the last word about himself. A man can choose to fulfill his *need to be*, he feels his power of going beyond functions and techniques to the core of being itself.

> We have now come to the center of what I called the ontological mystery, and the simplest illustration will be the best. To hope against hope that a person whom I love will recover from a disease which is said to be incurable is to say: It is impossible that reality in its inward depth should be hostile or so much as indifferent to what I assert is in itself a good. It is quite useless to tell me of discouraging cases or examples: beyond all experience, all probability, all statistics, I assert that a given order shall be re-established, that reality is on my side willing it to be so. I do not wish: I assert; such is the prophetic tone of true hope.[25]

This passage packs many elements of Marcel's thought into a very human illustration. The example of a friend hoping against all hope and against all the scientific reports that his beloved friend will still live and not die, that somehow there is something within being which (or who) joins me sympathetically in asserting this hope of life for my friend, this is the pool of experience within ourselves Marcel invites us to recollect and recover. What do we choose, or freely embrace, in such a situation? If, as we held previously, it is at the precise point of free choice that our real self is located, isn't it also true that in the situation just described my friend is inextricably present in me precisely as the focus of my hope and choice? And isn't it also the case that, in addition to my friend and me bound together in this hope and choice, I somehow take the mystery of reality that surrounds us as not hostile but supporting me, with me, in my hope for my friend?

Now a reality which hopes and loves and joins me in my freedom is no longer just another thing, but a personal reality, a supporting *Thou*, for my friendship. Thus the pattern of the wholing process through friendship grounded in a Being supporting that friendship begins to appear. To Marcel's mind, one penetrates to the inner core of *being* only when one freely chooses to cast one's lot *with* being as a Thou, as a surrounding but personal mystery that cooperates with me in my attempt to move from fragment, from emptiness, to fullness. Hence Marcel's expression: *esse est coesse* ("to be is to be with")—the preposition opening out to infinity itself for its object. To absolutize myself as a fragment is to remain empty and alone. To affirm and participate being, on the other hand, is to choose to be with being. To absolutize the fragment which is me is to betray being. Betrayal and fidelity, then, take on the meaning either of repudiating being as a personal Thou or of affirming myself as participating being as a Thou. So in this illustration, not analysis, we have moved from existence to being, and the access to being has been provided by intersubjectivity, the experience between persons, subjects, freely loving one another. It is specifically in the interpersonal experiences of fidelity, commitment, faith, and love that we get our insights into being, beyond existence and having.

Fidelity and availability among friends does not merely mean punctuality or constancy, the false pride one sometimes has in having performed externally what one promised a friend. Fidelity means being *present*, really *being with* one's friend. It is to receive the other into one's own being, to open whatever being one has toward the other. Hence Marcel talks of receiving as *active*; the welcoming of the other. There is significance in the fact that we receive our friend into our home, into our garden, not in a hotel room or the middle of the forest ordinarily, since these latter bear nothing of ourselves. Physical distance, and even death, has nothing to do with the mutual presence of friends in each other. Obversely, physical presence by itself does not automatically constitute *being with* the other. It is this idea of actively receiving the other into one's own being that Marcel keeps probing to bring out his meaning of fidelity. The following passages should help to clarify his point:

To encounter someone is not merely to cross his path but to be, for the moment at least, near to or with him. It means being a co-presence. . . . Thus the ambiguous term "receptivity" has a wide range of meanings extending from suffering or undergoing to the gift of self; for hospitality is a gift of what is one's own, oneself. . . . I hold in principle that reception, hence receptivity, can only be considered in connection with a certain readiness, or preordination. A person receives others in a room, in a house, if necessary in a garden, not on unknown ground or in a forest. . . . By this gift of self we are not concerned with filling up some empty space with an alien presence, but with having the other person participate in a certain reality, in a certain plenitude. To provide hospitality is truly to communicate of oneself to the other.[26]

Of course, this openness to the other is not without limit. What then is the limit? Marcel's thought probes deep into the concept of the self we presented and the limit he sets is that one never cease to be a *free subject*. It is my free reality, then, that I share with my friend, all the while maintaining myself always in the relationship as free and as a subject. And the supporting base for this relationship, that which enables me to commit myself to my friend even though I do not know how the future will affect either of us, is the "infinite credit" I extend to God as the surrounding Thou who is affirming the commitment I and my friend give each other.[27] To be faithful ever after to my friend is to hope that, with the supporting help of God, I will continue to use my freedom imaginatively and to channel creatively whatever changes occur toward upholding, not negating, our friendship. We see here Marcel's effort to hold God, my friend, and me in a delicate balance, each one a free subject all the while that there is interpenetration and co-presence of each in each to constitute a growing whole.

I belong to you; I give myself to you. This does not mean, at least in principle, that I am your slave. On the contrary, I freely put myself in your hands. It should be stressed that insofar as I accept being treated as a thing, I make myself a thing, and it is then significant to ask if I am not betraying myself. . . . Since I belong to you as you belong to me, I cannot wish to make you anything other than what you wish yourself. . . . Since I cease to belong to myself, it is not literally true to say that you belong to me; we transcend one another in the very heart of our love.[28]

We see now how availability, commitment, fidelity, the exigence-to-be, etc., are all synonymous in Marcel with love. And love is the individual, as a fragment, moving toward *being with* the other in the presence of God.

> We see then how intersubjectivity, which it is increasingly more evident is the cornerstone of concrete philosophy, is after all nothing but charity itself.[29]

If the counterpoint to Freud's thought in Marcel's explorations into the mystery of being is still unclear, the question of immortality in human friendship shows that the two men's conceptions of love are universes apart. For Marcel considers immortality, eternity, as the necessary context of genuine love. For him, the need to be and the need to be eternal are one and the same need.

> To say that one loves a person is to say, "Thou, at least, shalt not die." Because I love you, because I affirm you as being, there is something in you which can bridge the abyss that I vaguely call "death."[30]

In other words, communion between friends is not cancelled by death, since this is a reality beyond the level of mere existences and problems in the world of objects. In that world of objects, it is understandable that we can talk of here and there as actual distances separating objects. The objective reality of your boyfriend's rifle is present to him in Vietnam, for instance, in an entirely different way than you are present to him and he to you through love, even though a whole ocean separates you. Such distances do not touch, much less cancel the reality of your friendship. Does death then cancel your friendship? Shall we say that friendship is indeed preserved, since we continue to cherish a dead friend, but that all we cherish is merely a remembered and thus a fictitious reality? Or is our experience otherwise; namely, that at the core of our being, in our mysterious depth, we know it is still our friend who has died, whom we love? In this sense, to experience fullness at all, one must experience it precisely as a beyond.

> If death is the ultimate reality, value is annihilated in mere scandal, reality is pierced to the heart. Value can only be thought of as reality, if it is related to the consciousness of an immortal destiny.[31]

A writer on Marcel puts it this way:

> If death is able to polarize communion, it is only because it purifies it of this need for palpability. . . . If death purifies love, it is mainly by enabling it to shed all accoutrements of *having*; the dead beloved is no longer one who can be "had" at all. If he may still *be* for me, it is only because I exercise a kind of absolute forbearance in the face of physical absence.[32]

Without this aspiration for transcendence in human communion, this propulsion toward the eternal, the wholeness promised by love would not be real wholeness. The thought that death annihilates everything except the living would pierce the value of friendship to the heart, especially since genuine friendship moves toward greater and greater purity. And this motion toward purification, as we saw in the text above, is not annihilated but on the contrary intensified by death. That is why a character in one of Marcel's plays can say, "If there were only the living, Gisela, I think the earth would be altogether uninhabitable." Why? Because "I do not accede to the realm of being simply by freely accepting my situation, but by recognizing that the roots of my situation go down into the eternal. Being is the eternal dimension of my existential situation. Being is that to which I aspire."[33]

Is there any one concrete illustration of all these supposedly "concrete" Marcellian reflections? What good is it, someone may ask, to run for verification to characters in Marcel's own plays? He wrote those plays himself! This is a fair objection—provided, however, that it be made clear that in order to satisfy this demand for *verification* one is not being asked to resurrect and produce the dead to stand before the objector as convincing evidence. An objection that requires the impossible is not really an objection. What then? Will contacting the dead through various media, as is the wont nowadays, suffice? That might be one way. I doubt, however, that this is really what Marcel had in mind, though at one point in his life he was intrigued by such phenomena. More to the point perhaps is a most unusual book entitled *A Grief Observed* by an eminent man of letters, a very sensible and balanced individual, C. S. Lewis (1898-1963).

This was a little book C. S. Lewis wrote as a daily diary when he and his wife, whom he loved as much as his own life itself and possibly even more, found out she was stricken with a terminal illness. Each day brought the two of them nearer the day when they both knew she would have to leave him forever in death. In the pages of this diary can be found one of the most moving and beautiful records of human bravery and love in the face of the inescapable. As her days of life drew to an end, husband and wife made an unusual promise that many of us think about but rarely act upon. The Lewises believed in immortality and God, but they were not exempt from the universal human longing for verification spoken of by Hamlet, the desire to experience the dead coming back from "that undiscovered country from whose bourne no traveller returns." C. S. Lewis records:

> Once very near the end I said, "If you can—if it is allowed—come to me when I too am on my death bed." "Allowed!" she said. "Heaven would have a job to hold me; and as for Hell I'd break it to bits!" She knew she was speaking a kind of mythological language, with even an element of comedy in it. There was a twinkle as well as a tear in her eye. But there was no myth and no joke about the will, deeper than any feeling, that flashed through her.[34]

Well, did anything come of it? Did Mrs. Lewis come back to her husband, not in any *supernatural* way, nor yet through what we call mediums today, but precisely through that way of immortality we have seen Marcel attempting to express? The book is not a very long book; a reader can finish it in an hour or two. It may be best, then, to let C. S. Lewis present his case in its entirety to the reader, for he does record his wife's fulfillment to him of her dying promise.

We have said enough now to contrast views of man's wholing as taking place solely within the body or as continuing on, indeed as necessarily rooted in the eternal. Our next move, then, is to bring into more organized form the many threads and insights into human wholing found in Marcel. His "secondary reflection" is a disappointment to those who always seek rigorous progression of thought in a philosopher. Marcel's reply, of course, would be that such a demand is improper when it comes to probing the dimensions of being found within a person, a level of reality altogether diverse from the world of objects, of problems, of science. Still, it is desirable that some further analysis of the idea of love as interpersonal communion, and mutual copresence, be attempted. And it is just this attempt that we find in an excellent book, *The Experience of Love*, by Jules Toner, S.J.

3 TONER's *The Experience of Love*

Nearly everyone these days is aware of the vast and complicated mass of literature current on the topic of love.[35] Jules Toner's book, however, cuts through all that mass by posing the problem of love in terms of love's essence itself.[36] What is love *itself*, not this or that kind of love, but the radical love underlying all the variations of love encompassed in all that literature? Heretofore, Father Toner points out, all our theories of love have been *adjectival*; they have described and developed all sorts of love: natural, supernatural, mature, immature, romantic, sexual, parental, filial, benevolent, appetitive, courtly, Platonic, etc. The chart on the next page, for instance, is an attempt to outline the varieties of love theories as they are presented in Hazo, the most comprehensive book on the subject, published just as Toner's book went to press. Within this maze

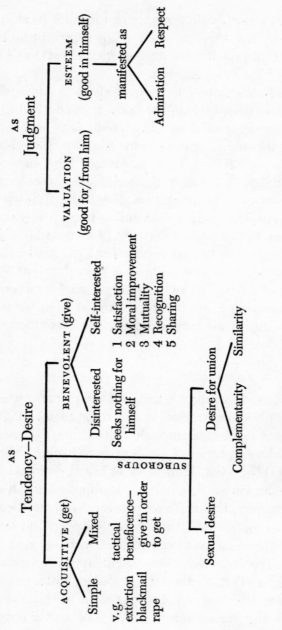

IDEA OF LOVE

As Tendency—Desire

ACQUISITIVE (get)
- Simple — v.g. extortion, blackmail, rape
- Mixed — tactical beneficence—give in order to get

BENEVOLENT (give)
- Disinterested — Seeks nothing for himself
- Self-interested — 1 Satisfaction, 2 Moral improvement, 3 Mutuality, 4 Recognition, 5 Sharing

SUBGROUPS
- Sexual desire
- Desire for union — Complementarity, Similarity

As Judgment

VALUATION (good for/from him)

ESTEEM (good in himself) — manifested as Admiration, Respect

Core terms for Tendency
1 Tendency in general
2 Acquisitive desire
3 Benevolent desire
4 Sexual desire
5 Desire for union

Core terms for Judgment
1 Esteem
2 Valuation

of theories, Toner seeks to bare the root concept of love itself (its substantival, not adjectival sense), though others might shrug off such a project as futile. Father Toner writes:

> It may fairly be required that, before adopting such a position, we first examine experience to see whether in those experiences called love we do not find certain essential elements, structured in certain constant ways . . . an examination of experience made to see whether there is not one radical element which is a necessarily constant in all love.[37]

Accordingly, he divides his book into two parts. First, he gives a dialectical survey of various love theories, analyzing each of them to the point where it can be shown to be not quite the irreducible, ultimate understanding of love Toner is seeking. For obvious reasons, we must limit ourselves here to mentioning only some high points of this first part. Father Toner has difficulty accepting Plato's version of love as an intermediate "means" to man's fullness in the world of Forms. For it seems incredible that love at its peak moment is love no longer, is in fact love's self-cancellation. He also rejects the rooting of all loves solely and exclusively within the body, as in Freud, since there are loves such as that of a St. Francis of Assisi which to all evidence transcended sex and the body. Again, he argues that the notion of love as joy calls for further refinement and precision, for love and joy are separable in many instances when grief sets in and love still endures and perdures. In reply to Eric Fromm's (1900–) well-known concept of love, that it is care and concern for the other in this other's own needs, Father Toner asks: why do you *care* for the other? Previously you did not care, now you do. Why? Doesn't this show that your care and concern arose precisely *because you love*?

If one then inquires further why you love, the answer cannot be because of the joy, or material possessions, or anything else that ensues from the relationship. For insofar as these things arise or result from the relationship, they are the effects, not love itself. This needs to be explained further. You desire, you are happy because of love. But this desire, this joy, etc., is not love itself. And if you say that material wealth made you love another, this would be an "implemental" love of sorts, a love of something good *for* someone, even if this someone turns out to be no other than the one who loves. Objects are desired, in other words, *for* a person you already love. Now it is this prior love Toner seeks to uncover. For this is radical love itself, which shows its ultimate character in the fact that we can only shrug our shoulders and point to it dumbly when we are asked why we love whomever we do love.

Suppose we say with Martin Buber (1878-1965) that this love is a participation, a sharing of two people in a common goal, a doing together of something the two enjoy. This still is not the irreducible understanding of love, since the two would not enjoy *doing* something together, unless prior to that (not necessarily prior in time but certainly in the order of dependence) there did not already exist an underlying *commonness in being*. Why, in other words, did we fall in love with this other person? Once again we cannot answer in terms of further causes. We can only assert the fact, thereby showing the ultimate ground for the variations of love; yet this ground itself is not a variation of something further. What then is this radical love? That is the question treated in the second part of Father Toner's book.

If the object of radical love is not something on the level of *having*, nor even on the level of *doing*, it follows that the object can only be the person's basic fundamental actuality, his personal act of being itself. It is to this personal actuality that a lover responds in radical love. In evoking such a response, this personal actuality reveals its nature to be an *appeal* for that response. Thus the basic path of radical love can be traced as a straight line—brushing aside all other incidentals—from personal actuality to personal actuality. Why one's love responds to one person rather than another, even though each person (or personal actuality) is an appeal for love, is a question Father

Toner does not raise and a point to be explored in the next chapter, when we come to the matter of communication and the human face. Toner simply holds that the beginning of radical love is not free; it occurs spontaneously, even if, to be fully human, it must be freely ratified or rejected.

How understand this response that is radical love? It is certainly not reducible to intellectual knowledge: we know many people we do not love radically. As we saw in Marcel, we are present to those we merely know and do not love in a vastly different way from those to whom we are present through love. Hence we recognize radical love as an affective presence of myself in the other and the other in me: I-in-me-you and I-in-you-me, to use Dante's words. Toner concedes that, put thus, there is indeed only a thin line dividing love from hate. For hate is also an affective presence, but a dissonant one, whereas radical love's presence is a consonant one.

Furthermore, radical love is not merely a giving *of* self, but self-giving, an accepting of the other into myself in one and the same act by which I give myself to the other affectively. Gifts and symbols and anything else attached to the person we love take on significance and meaning only because of this prior and basic union.

> In this experience, I am neither projecting my life into the other and so at root loving myself in him, nor am I so introjecting his life into me as to lose hold on my own distinct and unique self-identity. In fact, when the loved one's life as his is experienced as mine I become both more keenly alive to my own distinct and unique self and more keenly and reverently alive to the other in his distinct and unique otherness. For this is the very puzzling but clearly observable fact, that not only is participation in the beloved's life, as described, in direct ratio to the intensity and purity of radical love, but so also is the realization of the distinct and unique personal reality of both the loved and the lover.[38]

Christ's words "I was hungry and you gave me to eat" is an example of such distinction in identity. So is St. Paul's exclamation, "For me to live is Christ!" And we may consider what St. Augustine wrote about the death of his dearest friend in youth:

> Since I was his other self, I wondered the more that I could go on living when he was dead. The half of my soul—well has someone said this of his friend. For I felt my soul and his to have been one soul in two bodies. And therefore I dreaded life because I did not want to live mutilated. And therefore perhaps I dreaded death, lest the one I greatly loved should die entirely.[39]

This simultaneous identity and distinction through radical affection shows itself to be a coaffirmation of the beloved's act of being. Toner writes:

> In my act of being, I say me—not something to me or about me; and by saying me, I am. By being I exclaim myself; and by this exclaiming, I am myself in reality.[40]

It is this insight into radical love as a codeclaration of the beloved's personal act of being that enables Toner to explain the phenomenon common to lovers of exclaiming the beloved's name over and over again, whether in ecstatic tenderness or in the depth of grief.[41] It also explains how lovers can move toward their own destruction when they unite in a false declaration of themselves, a declaration that is out of touch with reality. As coaffirmation of the other, radical love can grow endlessly even toward the infinity of God, since a person's act of being is not an isolated reality but always within a network of relationships that stretch inexhaustibly toward divine knowledge itself. There is an unfathomable richness to the individual self, as we saw in Kierkegaard, which propels him toward an authentic relationship with the Infinite.

Finally, Toner shows how the structure of radical love is mutually intensifying through the communion of lovers. In a case where radical love is reciprocal, the other whom I love is precisely one who loves me, and I who love the other am precisely the I whom the other loves. There is thus a mutual refinding of each in each. Such is the life of love in communion. I love you loving me, and you love me loving you.

Nothing in all the material we have gone through to this point is as rich in implications for the part-toward-whole theme of this book as this notion of love's communion. Whether we talk of God and creatures, or simply of human persons among themselves engaged in the wholing process, the insight that I love all those who are present in someone I love, including myself, is as clear an example as any of what moving toward ever-growing wholeness means. Husband, wife, children, relations, friends, and so on, are all mutually in one another and beyond their own stage of fragmentation through the communion of love. And if, beyond Freud and his followers, one situates his ever-growing wholeness with others in the all-encompassing love of God, as do Marcel and Toner, the meaning-of-life question is diminished somewhat in its starkness, even while it remains a mystery. At any rate, the definition Father Toner gives of radical love should now be more understandable:

> Radical love is a response in which the lover affectively affirms the beloved for the beloved's self in himself, directly and explicitly in his personal act of being, implicitly in his total reality; by which affirmation the lover's personal being is consonantly present to and in the beloved and the beloved present to and in him; by which the lover affectively identifies with the loved one's personal being; by which in some sense the lover is the beloved.[42]

After reading Father Toner's book, however, there remains the question of his inadequate treatment of the beginnings of radical love. As we have seen, he simply states that radical love begins spontaneously, that it is not free. But why this is so, he does not even bother to wonder. His book is built rather on the manifestations of this love *after* it has begun. Not once is there an explicit mention of man as a fragment impelled toward the whole. Or, put another way, why is a person, any person, intrinsically lovable? The same question cannot be raised regarding objects; for these, as we saw, are loved only derivatively, always *for* someone. I think it is here, perhaps, that our theme of human life as inclined toward wholing can help to complete Toner's otherwise excellent philosophizing on love.

Our explanation would be that personal actuality is intrinsically lovable because its nature is that of a part seeking wholeness, dramatically illustrated in the Aristophanic myth of the *Symposium*. "It can readily be said that the individual is the one in a fragmented state," Marcel has written.[43] We have seen how this "fragment" is a being that tends all the while toward wholeness through interpersonal relationship with others: *esse est coesse*. It seems sensible, then, to say that two individuals, in tending toward wholeness, relate to each other as a desirable and growing whole. A personal act of being, in other words, is intrinsically lovable because it is the only reality that fits into the wholing process to which every man is impelled. But if we press the point even more specifically and ask why radical love happens to this or that individual—and not just to anyone, since every man has a personal act of being—we have reached the point where we are seemingly at a loss for an explanation. Perhaps this is why, on this very point, even Plato in the Aristophanic myth found himself unable to go beyond that myth: "When a pair chance on each other, an amazing friendship blazes forth which does not appear to be the desire of lover's intercourse, but which the soul of either evidently desires and cannot tell, and of which she has only a dark and doubtful presentiment."

Needless to say, one can only love someone who is within the ambit of his consciousness. Without being "offered," so to speak, to the other's consciousness, the intrinsic lovability of a person cannot be responded to by that other. Of course, the way of "offering" oneself can be as extensive as individual ingenuity and circumstances. It could conceivably take the form of simply choosing to be in a certain place at a certain time with a certain group of people. Yet even this, in Maurice Nédoncelle's thought on the matter, is to freely decide to expose one's countenance to the possible response of love, no

matter how one-sided or secret and nonmutual the love ignited
may appear to be.

> . . . he has not willed me by name, he has not turned toward me as a
> result of a special decision, but he has given himself to the world, he
> has willed this in willing to display his activity and allow his per-
> sonality to be glimpsed there. Thus it is that he has caused his being
> to shine in my own. . . . To be in the world is to be a minimum of
> goodness publicly exposed. A countenance that appears is a reality
> surrendered, a secret cautiously unveiled. The person is an expres-
> sion and a role: he soon learns to calculate his effects or to poison
> the atmosphere. But in the beginning he is unaware of his grimaces
> and is all freshness and trust. Love is always watching for this initial
> moment, and that is why it is born in mutuality even though it must
> often sink into solitude.[44]

This passage from Nédoncelle nicely complements Toner's
analysis of love. At the same time, it makes explicit something
that has so far been only implicit in all the preceding pages,
namely, the role of the human "face" in the process of wholing.
Take any thinker we have mentioned up to now, any idea
on the meaning-of-life problem we have encountered, and invariably you notice how they all presuppose a face-to-face relationship among the participants of the wholing process. If
face-to-face means anything, however, it means *communication*.
Hence love, communion, communication, and the *face* are all
linked together. But now we must bring them all together in
the light of some crucial problems that beset all of us today:
the breakdown of communication and alienation among friends;
and more positively, the face-to-face wholing process of married love.

THE FACE, HONESTY, AND BEYOND

It is all very well for Philip Rieff's "therapeutic man" to be seemingly so universally permissive while he goes about the business of living life to the full. But sooner or later, in an age of mass media, diverging ideologies have a way of cleaving their differences into personal relationships, and universal permissiveness shrivels up quickly when alienation sets in. So today we live with the phenomenon of breakdown in communication: in church, neighborhood, families, etc. What are we to make of our wholing process against this sad picture?

We can start by noting our instinctive reaction to turn our faces *away* from those with whom we want no interpersonal relationships, for whatever cause, and *toward* those whom we perceive to be potential friends and, as such, wholesome influences in our lives. In whatever direction we face, we face that way because of a decision on our part to communicate or not to communicate with someone we perceive to be either a poor or good participant in our wholing process. And yet a wholing process that excludes others is obviously a contradiction! What then are we to make of the link between language, the face, human goodness, and the infinite potential of friendships built on this goodness?

1 LANGUAGE AND THE FACE

In *Totality and Infinity*, Emmanuel Levinas, a contemporary French thinker, advances the startling contention that we grasp the notion of infinity itself through the unique mediation of the human face.[1] Most everything else in our experience can be *totalized*, meaning it can be stuck into our customary categories without loose edges or lingering traces of mystery. But the human face is singularly different. The faces of people around us, "the stranger, the widow and the orphan," escape containment by our usual organizing categories. That elusive dimension of the human "self" revealed somehow in the face is yet never contained within the limits of the familiar where we find it. Even in the extreme situation, in the "pure experience" of war, when surrender to another's will is gotten by force of steel, there still remains that unbounded interiority paradoxically affirmed in the very concept of "prisoner." The prisoner's interiority constantly breaches the captor's impositions, no matter how ruthless the captor. Without utterance, even in this barbaric relationship, the face still demands that contact be made with the center of freedom within the prisoner. Yet force, violence, and threats are all unavailing for the establishment of this contact.

What we are essentially saying is that the elemental requisite for response, both initially and in the ensuing stages of growth in a human whole, is the *trust* evoked by the face of the other, the stranger, as he approaches to communicate. More primordial and anterior to language itself, this face-to-face contact is vital. In that moment, language is born.[2] In that moment, if successfully sustained, language dwells, moves, and has its being. Miming and mimicking, already languages themselves, point back to this basic life of trust in the face. Put another way, language establishes itself through the overlapping of body gestures between speakers, as another French thinker, the late Maurice Merleau-Ponty (1908-1961), phrased it:

What I communicate with primarily is not "representations" or thought, but a speaking subject, with a certain style of being and with the "world" at which he directs his aim. . . . Our view of man remains superficial as long as we fail to find, beneath the chatter of words, the primordial silence, and as long as we do not describe the action which breaks this silence. The spoken word is a gesture, and its meaning a world.[3]

Hence, too, language breaks down, goes dead, once this primordial trust is broken. The corpses of such deaths in communication take many forms. We see them in a speaker's flight from language to mocking sounds, or else to a silence designed to snuff out any lingering breath in the trusting relation that formerly effected and nourished communication. In Levinas' incisive analysis:

Thus silence is not a simple absence of speech; speech lies in the depths of silence like a laughter perfidiously held back. It is the inverse of language, like a laughter that seeks to destroy language. It is the situation created by those derisive beings communicating across a labyrinth of innuendoes which Shakespeare and Goethe have appear in their scenes of sorcerers where speech is anti-language, and where to respond would be to cover oneself with ridicule.[4]

For a concrete illustration, we can turn perhaps to the university, ideally the most civil of places amidst the discontents of civilization. On a recent television show, six radical professors were interviewed. There they were, strangers to most of the audience, eventually getting to the point of their substantive vision of America as she should *not* be: filled by rampant consumerism, racism, corruptive and corrosive competitiveness, inhumanity, etc. And then of America as she should be: distributing goods "rationally" through cooperatives instead of through the motive of corporate profit and so equalizing, for instance, the pay of janitors and professors; food should be free, hospitals free, anything in fact American society has enough of should be free. But the high point of the show came when a man from the floor, in his fifties, expressed his agreement with the professors' humanistic ideals and then posed a question, clear and simple: How, just *how*, did the professors plan to carry out this "national distribution" for 200 million Americans?

Skilled in words, the professors talked back, but never really answered the question. And then, just seconds before the end of the program, a philosophy professor who had come across as a candid but by no means inconsiderate radical, admitted the impossibility of answering the question. But his counterquestion was exquisite. He swung his chair on stage to face the questioner standing on the floor and facing him. "Isn't it more important," asked the radical professor, "since you and I agree on the ideal of caring for the hungry and poor, that you and I get down and work together immediately, now, toward achieving that goal, instead of waiting for agreement on every detail of the plan? You see, there *are* poor people starving, right now, in the midst of more than enough food to go around!" The questioner, still facing the professor, replied: "I'm sure I can work with you, sir, but not with those others around you!" On this bombshell, charged with all sorts of philosophical implications, the program ended. It was a graphic dramatization of today's problems, yet with the seeds within it of some solutions.

The last professor was clearly of the same political stripe as the other radicals around him. Moreover, he had a facial tic that was mercilessly obvious during those inescapable camera close-ups—clearly, his was not the handsomest face on the panel! All six radicals were equally eloquent, equally gifted intellectually. What then was it in the last speaker which effected that unequal response in the questioner, who was a stranger to them all? Why did he side with this last professor and explicitly repudiate the others? He *heard* one, but not the rest, when all of them had really been saying the same thing. Why? Subtlety? No, there was little subtlety among the angry radicals when they delivered their message of charity for all. Why then?

Could *face* have played a crucial role in the situation? Among those faces of strangers, one face simply *communicated* and was gifted with a response; the rest of those faces alienated him—just as, in the lived-world, we turn away from each other and look elsewhere when two consciousnesses are unhappy with each other to the point of deafness. Then, for the alienated parties, the mere physical sight of the other rings down a curtain of deafness that no increase in vocal volume can hope to penetrate. Only the discovery of a *third face*, the mediator (or his equivalent in the shape of an event so shaking as to alter the two unhappy countenances), can raise communication from the dead back to life, and nourish and sustain it in his own face for as long as the alienated parties are yet unable to hear and look at each other.

Clearly, we are not taking "face" here in its literal, purely physical meaning. Nor yet in the meaning, supposedly peculiar to the Chinese, of "losing face"—something we are all coming to realize these days is a rather widespread trait among humans of every race, color, or creed. And certainly, handsomeness is not essential to our meaning of face. How often has the distorted face of a stranger in a strange land evoked a compassion that overrode any initial recoil! No, "face" here refers not so much to one's physical appearance as it does to *something appearing* in the whole man which yet concentrates with special light on the physical face and uses this latter as its most effective point of unveiling. Rollo May, among others, points out in *Love and Will* how a man's whole body bespeaks—is simply the locus of appearance of—that deeper something (or lack of it?) that shapes all his actions and patterns all his gestures:

> Even more interesting is the body as language of intentionality. It not only expresses intentionality; it *communicates* it. Not only in the therapeutic hour but in real life as well, our communication has, much more than we are aware of it, the subtle character of the dance, the meaning communicated by virtue of the forms we continually create by bodily movements.[5]

This embodied meaning of life for a man, appearing out of the mystery that he himself is, what a person most deeply *cares* for or goes *toward* amidst life's Sisyphean cycle of going and returning, May takes as "intentionality." And I would add that this intentionality indeed converges somehow toward the ambience of his *face*, though of course this is not to say that we know a man's character by his face in a clear and distinct way. The interiority and immeasurable depth of a human being prevents any such clear disclosure as can be had of objects that are in a very real sense all surface. Nevertheless, in a way proper to the mysterious reality of a person, the self one has forged and become as he lived his life's meaning somehow reflects in the face, and thereby gives birth to language.

But does not meaning demand an other to whom the meaning is directed? Indeed it does. It would be odd to find a "fragmented" individual successfully substantializing to himself a self-enclosed meaning of life! On the other hand, it might be nice but it would surely be folly for many of us to put on a we're-all-friends pose. So neither group or solitary exclusivity, nor a posturing of universal friendship, will do. How does one steer between this sort of Scylla and Charybdis? If, as May points out, we can only see in others what we ourselves have previously perceived and conceived, then for one to see the stranger's face, to hear him, one already must have within himself the same meaning (intentionality, virtue) he perceives, if only vaguely, in the stranger. A meeting of faces, therefore, whenever and wherever it occurs, is indeed a recognition of deep calling unto deep.[6] Then how do we avoid the fate of a few in a charmed circle, happy in being alike but cut off from growth as they cordon off their unlikes? How can we move on to an explanation that encompasses the actuality of a mediator making contact and driving home a message to two faces incapable of receiving the selfsame from each other in a direct face-to-face posture? How understand, in short, that third face, that focus of reconciliation for opposites?

At this point it seems imperative to go beyond May's concept of intentionality as will giving definite shape to one's life. Obviously, virtue and/or intentionality is not a simple, but rather a many-splendored, thing—though it has long been debated whether in fact all human virtues can be ultimately reduced to one.[7] This question gave rise to various portraits of the orderly enchainment of virtues among themselves, sometimes (as in Aquinas) with charity functioning as the architectonic, unifying factor. But prescinding from the question of how or whether virtues are plural, what is pertinent for our discussion here is the consideration that though a single virtue may be indeed indivisible (one cannot be "almost chaste"), yet in its overlapping with other virtues toward the crowning point (e.g., Aquinas' face-to-face fullness of charity in the "beatific vision") it admits of more or less actualization. We meet men, for example, who are more kind than just, more courageous than sympathetic, more chaste than generous, etc. The point is that while intentionality usually is predominantly *one* (hence a person has a *characteristic* face), nevertheless it is commingled with the transcendence of this very characteristic itself in the infinity of the face, which, as we said, escapes categorization. Could the ground of this transcendence then be lesser intentionalities clustered around the predominant one, lesser intentionalities actualized in a person enough to be somehow open to the perception and trust of the stranger? We might even say that the cluster of lesser intentionalities in the two possibly overlap, even as their predominant ones repel each other as unlikes (as in our example above of the radical professor and the questioner). But here we have a thought that requires interruption: How can intentionalities or virtues, whether dominant or not, be mutually repulsive? Can a good oppose a good?

On this point G. W. Leibniz's (1646-1716) remark that simple perfections are compatible with each other may help us out.[8] No need here to go into the sophisticated concept of a simple perfection; the point is simply that virtues are perfections and thus not opposed but compatible with each other. Mutual repulsion between two individuals with the same outstanding virtue, however, may be explained by suggesting that one reads the other's virtue (correctly or not) as a threat instead of a support to his own. Why? Not because the virtue itself causes such a reading, but because its surrounding circumstances do. Take the movie *Bridge Over the River Kwai*, the story of two individuals fiercely and tenaciously militaristic but in opposite camps. Neither one allows the other the slightest inch if he can help it, yet one senses the growth of a profound understanding and even admiration between the two. Am I saying, then, that all human life is a warfare and that this causes such misreadings of others? No. But I do say that to the extent human life is lived at certain times in circumstances *like war*, virtues even of the same sort among individuals can collide. We see this often enough between husband and wife, between the proverbial in-laws, between parents and child, friend and friend, etc. We shall see in the following section how the "maximizing of one's being" as a universal characteristic of all organisms also throws light on this matter. Suffice it to say for the moment that unless the third face, the mediator, appears, communication is the first casualty of such collisions and the last state is worse than the first.

To resume the positive thrust of our reflections, let us return to the question of overlapping lesser intentionalities between strangers as a ground for transcendence. We can see how a certain infinity appears in the potentials of these clusters, as circles of friends, otherwise closed to each other, are fissured *through mediators* outward to strangers, who in turn can themselves open out to others again and effect further and further mediation. We see, in other words, how circles of friends widen, since in actual circumstances one is constantly discovering how both the predominant and lesser intentionalities in every man are of an endless variety and richness.

Furthermore, a person himself is not necessarily aware of the possibilities rooted in his conscious and predominating intentionality. Only the test of actual challenges and crises will reveal the best or the worst in us, our unknown strengths and weaknesses. This is all of a piece with the fusion of being and becoming we saw earlier in considering the nature of the self as free. Encounter with the stranger outside often reveals the stranger inside ourselves, namely, the pattern of choices we have formed without our explicit notice. As one writer puts it:

> The reason for the essential adumbrativeness in all social reality is the recognition that the individual is, in some measure, a stranger to himself, that each of us knows himself only in aspects, and that every person is therefore a partial repression both of his accomplishments and his possibilities.[9]

Finally, with these considerations of communication and friendship in mind, it is worth remarking that we have a greater propensity to trust the other, the stranger, when there is joy in his face. This requisite for joy is something one finds even in Camus, the philosopher of the absurd. He describes how Sisyphus' face must have looked as that giant turned around at the mountaintop to start his descent to the lower world, there to start pushing the boulder uphill again, eternally. "A face that toils so close to stone is already stone itself!" exclaims Camus. Amidst the oppressive stones of his native North African shores, he cries for defiance and "revolt" against the massive boulders of meaninglessness by raising one's face above them "to the sky"—where laughter and swirling desires revitalize one's face. "That secret and that rapture we ask of faces," he writes, "can also be given by stone!"[10] Can it? Have we seen any other views of man's being and becoming that indeed provide grounds for joy as one undergoes the setbacks and betrayals ordinarily included in the wholing process of life? We shall take this question up again in our concluding chapter. For now let me simply remark that one may admire such laughter without necessarily being attracted by it.

Yet other views, too, invite our reflection. Marcel, for instance, has pointed to the intimate connection between satisfaction, so prevalent in a technological age, and *taedium vitae* and faithlessness.

> But of course this does not mean that a philosophy of attestation and faith need necessarily be a cult of moral pain. The quality which is furthest from satisfaction is not pain, but joy. . . . Satisfaction is something that happens within doors, in a *closed* creature; but joy can only unfold beneath the open sky.[11]

There, in Camus and Marcel, we have a contrast between a philosopher who believes only in this world, and another who believes that the human spirit must make "herself penetrable to the transcendent yet inward action without which she is nothing."

But what if one can accept neither Camus' forced laughter nor Marcel's joy in the transcendent? What of those embittered moments when neither the massive world around us nor the sky beyond reveals anything to our sight but simply other defeats to come?

To my way of thinking, there is much beauty and wisdom in the way Cervantes portrays the end of Don Quixote. There is a complete reversal of minds as the despairing idealist listens to his realistic servant, who has learned well the art of looking beyond the windmills of the mind.

> Turning to Sancho, he said: "Forgive me, friend, for perverting thy understanding, and persuading thee to believe that there were, and still are, knight-errants in the world." "Alas! good sir," replied Sancho, "do not die, I pray you; but take my advice and live many years; for the greatest folly a man can commit in this world is to give himself up to death, without any good cause for it, but only from melancholy. Rise, and let us be going to the field dressed like shepherds, as we agreed to do. Who knows but behind some bush or other we may find the Lady Dulcinea disenchanted as fine as heart can wish; your worship must have seen in your books of chivalry that nothing is more common than for one knight to unhorse another, and that he who is vanquished today may be the conqueror tomorrow."[12]

I think it not mere coincidence but a genuine achievement of human wisdom that this finest passage from Cervantes should make the same point we heard Dewey make in our first chapter ("the longest lane turns sometime") about the essentially mixed and unpredictable condition of human affairs. What is needed, Dewey said, is "measure, relation, ratio, knowledge of the comparative tempos of change."

2 CONDITIONS FOR HONESTY

We shift now to take a hard look at another problem communication presents today: the problem of honesty. No human whole can be built without face-to-face communication, as we have just seen. Yet no whole built on dishonest communication among the participants can long endure either, for to be dishonest is by definition to be unreal. The question is whether *total* honesty, really "telling it like it is" as the contemporary expression has it, is the only way to build life's wholes. Since "telling it like it is" was the motivating force in Freud's life and work, perhaps we can be guided in our discussion by his thoughts about honesty. He tells this "just-suppose" story:

> A number of ladies and gentlemen in good society have planned to have a picnic. The ladies have arranged among themselves that if one of them wants to relieve a natural need, she will announce that she is going to pick flowers. Some malicious person, however, has got wind of the secret and has printed on the programme which is sent around to the whole party: "Ladies who wish to retire are requested to announce that they will pick flowers."[13]

The embarrassment that ensues, the regrouping to reword the statement, and the malicious person's ruthless effort to reveal and verbalize any and every repression he finds—all these are premises to Freud's conclusion:

> no lady will avail herself of this flowery pretext or other similar formulas which, in the same way, will be seriously compromised. What will be the result? The ladies will admit their natural needs without shame, and none of the men will object.[14]

This deceptively simple "story" is in fact quite a skillful illustration of Freud's analytic. The pleasure principle and its repression, the reality principle and the ego, the power of fantasy and therapy, etc., are all there. Our interest, though, is not in these technicalities but rather in using Freud's thought to unravel the problem of honesty in interpersonal relationships.

Honesty is a great word in these days of mass media and the "face," and phoniness is the new mortal sin. We are told that everyone must "tell it like it is" if he is to achieve truly wholesome relationships. Does this mean that everyone must tell *everything* like it is? The question is not unrelated, obviously, to the trend toward public nudity. And yet it is interesting to note how, in actual discussions, no one seriously defends the possibility of telling everything like it is in day-to-day living. So perhaps it makes more sense to rephrase the question this way: Why is not telling everything like it is *not necessarily being phony*? Or, to put it in terms of building human wholes, is it possible to relate to the other constructively without having to tell him everything like it is, every time, and this without being a phony? What, in other words, should be the controlling attitudes behind the constructive and destructive uses of honesty? What are the conditions for *not* telling everything like it is, at least some of the time?

We return to Freud. Certainly, his ideal was the honest man who tells it like it is, on the supposition that one knows, or has engaged therapeutic technique in order to know, things as they are.[15] Yet, Freud was equally certain that it is impossible for men to remain civilized without practicing repression.[16] Repression goes hand in hand with civilization and its highest products: saints, heroes, art forms, government, the life of thought, society itself or, on the most basic level, the definition of maturity we saw previously as "ability to postpone gratification." But how can we achieve the ideal of honesty if repression is of the very essence of a civilized, mature man? One cannot, in choosing honesty, simply say "so much the worse for civilization"; without restraints, man's pleasure principle would ultimately implode on itself. And so we are back to the question: How honest can you be, how can you tell all, if you may not trespass beyond certain limits under pain of abandoning civility for barbarism, the surest way to self-extinction?

Is the "malicious person" in Freud's "just-suppose" story a barbarian or not? Freud presents him approvingly, all the while maintaining the necessity of repression. Is this consistent? Here we are forced back to a controversy that really controls all the questions we have been raising: namely, the question of whether man is basically benign. Freud did not think so. Even a quick reading, for instance, of Paul Roazen's account of the "curious triangle" between Freud, Lou Salomé, and Victor Tausk—one of Freud's brilliant students whom the master eventually drove to suicide—shows Freud's characteristically defensive posture even among his friends.[17] What view ought one take, therefore, of the age-old controversy whether human nature is basically good or vicious?[18]

There is a precision to this controversy recently made by Ernest Becker. After listing contemporary supporters of the Hobbesian and the Rousseauvian views of man, and after having offered his own corrections to the popular notion that Rousseau's man was naturally "noble," Becker argues that man is born *neutral*. (Indeed, Becker maintains that this was Rousseau's own position.) Subsequent accretions of "uncritical allegiances to different sources of sustaining power" are what cause a human being to veer more to one side than the other in the nobility/savagery dichotomy.

> The uniqueness of man is that, with reason and thought, he might have a different destiny if he could but see through his Oedipus or early training, and come to identify the unconscious rooting of his own sense of self. This is what Freud taught us and this is precisely where he and Rousseau meet.[19]

Becker lines up contemporary authors such as Daniel Bell, Edward Shils, Talcott Parsons, and Neil Smelsen in opposition to

C. Wright Mills, John R. Seeley, and Edgar Friedenberg ("the reviews they write of each other's books!") in the Hobbes/Rousseau division, and then goes on to say that "human evil springs from the ground of restless striving that characterizes all organisms." Specifically:

> People are not born with drives of hate or aggression, but rather man as an energy-converting and purposive organism seeks the maximization of his own being, of his own sense of self. When neutral organisms seek to expand their self-feeling and to extend their control, they must need to do so in some way in competition with or at the obvious expense of their fellows. And this makes them seem "motivated" by anti-social desires. But the ontological ground is neutral, not in itself destructive. This is the important point.[20]

A fine insight into the whole controversy. But if it is true that man is basically a neutral organism, isn't it also true that he can't escape from "sources of sustaining power" that are beyond his control? One recalls Leo Tolstoy (1828-1910), who agonized over Christ's injunction to "resist not evil" and wondered whether it was something in his own life that made the saying seem so impossible. He pinpointed his trouble thus:

> I had drunk it with my mother's milk insensibly from earliest childhood. . . . I was taught to respect the institutions that protected me from violence and evil and to regard them as sacred. . . . I was taught to judge and to inflict punishment.[21]

How does one move beyond this Tolstoyan brooding over the inescapable imprint we receive from our institutions to a view of man in his depths? Here a thought from Camus may help advance our analysis. Camus had no illusions about men being fundamentally good and yet he could say: "on the whole, men are more good than bad."[22] And again, on the last page of his novel *The Plague*, we find him musing that when all is said and done "there are more things to admire in men than to despise"—and this even *after* the sources of sustaining power have made their impressions. This is a decisive consideration we need to exploit, but for completeness we should recall again here and explain some points on the notion of self we presented in our second chapter.

We said there that "the man himself" is his power of free choice; then we showed how this was not something substantialized in isolation from the rest of man but rather continuous with his whole being, since the will is continuous with the intellect and the senses. And this is consistent with the Thomistic position that man, with all his social roles and self in depth (so to speak), is just one actuality in himself with one act of existing (the "personal act of being," as we saw in our section on Toner). A Thomist would likewise say that this one act is received directly in the vital principle, the soul, and through the soul affects everything in man that is not the soul.[23] Reason and animality are mutually interpenetrative of each other in man, precisely through the one human actuality present in him. Thus when a man through reflective reason and will overcomes his sense appetites, one part of him ("pure reason," surely a fantastic fiction) does not stand triumphant, so to speak, with its foot on the neck of another subdued part of him (an equally fictitious "pure animal") and vice versa. (Descartes, for all his theorizing on the passions and the soul, would surely concede this in the light of his own experience of fathering an illegitimate child![24]) Reason dominant or defeated is shot through with animality, and animal inclination at its moment of consummation against reflective reason is saturated with a *human* quality.

There is no need to complicate this further by bringing in, at this point, one's religious faith.[25] If one has the life of faith, this again is not separate but all of a piece with the one human being there is, even though the theoretical aspects of this union are well-nigh insurmountable, as a careful reading of the medieval thinkers demonstrates.[26] Hence one should not talk of one's moral norm as *either* reflective reason, *or* emotions, *or* intuition, *or* faith, each by itself, etc. Man's reflective self-presence unites all these in his one being. Ultimately, then, it is a question of how one chooses which of these powers will be given primacy in the context of making a moral decision, the full play of man's "co-natural" prudence.[27] To repeat, there is only one man with various roles or levels of operation unified in and through the self in him, as we saw previously.

But to return to our discussion of honesty and the question whether one can tell it like it is all the way down to this depth that is the man himself. We have suggested that a key text is Camus' statement that, when all is said and done, and admitting all the wickedness in men, there is still more to admire than to despise in them; more actually, and more potentially, in the sense of a growing goodness or humanization of the other. It does seem possible at least to unravel the problem of honesty, of telling everything like it is, on the basis of this optimistic view of "human nature"; without this optimism the problem becomes well-nigh insoluble. For phoniness would then be equated with legitimate (because necessary) self-defense against the malicious other. Hence it seems sensible to move beyond the either/or dichotomy to Becker's *neutral* man, and then on to Camus' *admirable* man. For this something admirable in the other becomes my basis for relating to him, not in defense but in hope. And this hopeful view of the other can provide a key to both the theoretical and practical aspects of the problem of honesty.

Suppose one asks why we should take this optimistic view of man, given so many empirical evidences to the contrary? What then? I would answer in two ways. First, empirical evidence goes both ways; it shows not only the viciousness but also the nobility in man, and so provides room for optimism. Secondly, one can point back to the Catholic tradition as we saw it in D'Arcy's *The Mind and Heart of Love*, a tradition of optimism about the authentic role of human effort in the process of wholing, in partnership with divine grace. Man is not just nothing and God everything in the moral enterprise. Man in partnership with God is able to shape himself into a morally good being. And it is to this hopeful view of man that one can look for a solution to the problem of honesty.

For to hope is to admit the presence of counterforces. And aware of such forces, hope cannot be itself unless it also moves toward their humanization. Yet it doesn't make sense to think that such counterforces can be humanized overnight, in one continuous outpouring that tells everything like it is all the way down to the "man himself," a goal that sometimes seems to be the aim of sensitivity sessions. Rather, prudential calculation as to how much one can "tell it like it is" to the other, always with the hopeful view of providing the proper climate for growth in him of what is admirable over what is despicable (what else could "humanization" mean?), mediates the tension between honesty and repression, between being or not necessarily being phony whenever one chooses not to tell everything. And to foster the admirable in the other, to humanize, to provide a climate conducive to human growth—are these not in the last analysis really the human wholing process itself?

In the "just-suppose" story with which we began this discussion, Freud was certainly not against manners and social finesse as such. Rather we can interpret the story as meaning the ladies had reached a point where niceties were a hindrance rather than a help toward drawing forth the admirable in others; in other words, the distinction between healthy and unhealthy repression. How to turn the prudential trick, of course, demands deftness, sometimes exquisite deftness![28] "How can I tactfully tell a good friend," someone asks, "that the torn and filthy dishrag she keeps lovingly draped over the kitchen faucet is enough to kill a person's appetite? Should I quietly remove it and hope she takes the hint?"

Needless to say, prudential calculation can also call on occasion for telling it like it is all the way, even with what seem to be ultimately destructive effects on human wholes one has patiently built up to that point. Yet even here, one should distinguish the rage from the hope aspect, no matter how residual and clouded over this latter may be in such situations of ulti-macy: the almost desperate hope that the admirable in the other may still emerge by the use of the last remaining tactic. Thus Robert Lifton shows how mockery of all sorts, including ultimate forms, could help "expand the field of possibilities" (he borrows the phrase from Sartre).[29] He uses rebelling students at Columbia and their slogan "Up Against the Wall!" as an illustration. To interpret this slogan, Lifton moves beyond the Freudian bent that would see in it simply an Oedipal indication of the sons' wish to replace their fathers, to a position that sees in mockery a constructive instrument for change, an instrument reflectively able to mock even its own mockery for effectiveness.

> The phrase is a way of playing with an image of ultimate violation and retribution for that violation. The tone is less one of irreconcilable rage than one of taunting ridicule and mimicry. And the continuous reversals, the switches between victimizer and victim, ultimately mock not only the whole social order and its linguistic taboos. They mock the mocking phrase itself.[30]

We can sum up all we have said as follows. Because I prudently decide to hold back from "telling it like it is," I am not thereby phony—at least not necessarily so. The self in every man, beyond the social roles he necessarily plays, has hopeful and despicable aspects. The attitude consistent with the theme of wholing we have advocated all along is to fix one's gaze on this hopeful depth in the other, to believe that this is the richer part of him, and that the meaning of life (whatever this intentionality may be for one) should certainly include this humanization process. One does this by overcoming what is despicable in both oneself and the other, and this really comes down to encouraging the growth of the admirable in the other. Repression then takes on the positive aspect of *constructive hope*, without which the face-to-face process of building human wholes, in our day of instant and mass communication, cannot hope to succeed.

THE WHOLING OF MARRIED LOVE

No interpersonal relationship embodies the wholing process so directly and so intensely as a successful husband-wife relationship. Accordingly, we must face up to the challenges flung at marriage today and probe this idea of wholing to see its relationship to marriage. Moreover, since it is in the Catholic tradition we find a rigorous position on the permanence and indissolubility of marriage, we would do well to cast our discussion against that tradition as background.

A frequent objection today, for example, against the Catholic notion of marriage is that it absolutizes something that cannot be absolutized: namely, one's future life. How do I know what I will be a few years from now, and what circumstances will do to change me?[1] If I do not know my future, how can I bind myself by a promise to remain one definite, permanent sort of person, as the absolute character of marriage and the marriage vows seem to require? Even prescinding from the technicalities of dissolubility in the Church's canon law, how should one understand that unconditional commitment?

Doesn't it seem that all one can really ever promise a friend is one's best efforts in the future? And yet few, even today, seem to want to incorporate the phrase "to do my best" as a substitute for the traditional absolute promise in the marriage ceremonies. A coed voiced a perhaps typical reaction to such a suggestion when she said, "I'd turn and throw the bouquet in his face if, to the questions, 'do you etc.' during the ceremony, he replied, 'I'll do my best!' " That leaves us with three alternatives: (1) simply disregard and do away with marriage; (2) simply reaffirm the traditional absolute character of marriage; (3) recast the understanding of marriage as absolute indeed, but in a context of dynamic wholing between husband and wife. This last is the position I adopt in this chapter. For brevity's sake, I will treat the first two positions simultaneously, since the second is usually what provokes the first alternative.

Shall we then discard marriage? Everyone knows of instances where married partners have gone sour on each other, to put it mildly, and yet go on living together for the sake of the children, or for economic reasons, etc. To continue to call such relationships true marriages certainly seems absurd, since the substance of the relationship is gone and only the facade remains. On the other hand, it may be precisely such situations that highlight the need for the marriage promise, a point well made in Thornton Wilder's (1897–) play *The Skin of Our Teeth*, when Antrobus prepares to leave Mrs. Antrobus after five thousand years of marriage for a wild fling with Sabina. Mrs. Antrobus reminds him:

> I didn't marry you because you were perfect. I didn't even marry you because I loved you. I married you because you gave me a promise. That promise made up for your faults. And the promise I gave you made up for mine. Two imperfect people got married and it was the promise that made the marriage. And when our children were growing up, it wasn't the house that protected them; and it wasn't our love that protected them—it was that promise.[2]

It is grossly unfair to characterize even the Catholic tradition on marriage as focusing so narrowly on the promise as to make love altogether peripheral. But Wilder's text is surely to the point in our discussion about soured marriage partners who, for one reason or another, are still trying to hold together. Mrs. Antrobus' words are enlightening, for they show that all other considerations for holding together adduced by either one or both partners are really secondary to the *promise*. And marriage vows have, in fact, traditionally stood as *the* essence of marriage, since the exchange and consummation of the vows, in the traditional view, marry the partners to each other "till death." What can be said of this view?

First, it would be silly to defend the hypocrisy of a man and woman who married, who now hate each other, and who yet, for convenience of some kind or other, still put up a facade of marriage. Clearly, *love*, not the promise, is the essence of marriage. The problem rather is how to understand the promise in relation to that love, for the promise itself cannot stand for love, Wilder's words to the contrary notwithstanding.

Secondly, we can say that the traditional notion of a consummated marriage leaves much to be desired. One theologian has pointed out that whatever marriage consummation may be, it seems erroneous to believe the *prima nox* ("first night") interpretation of it: namely, that once the marriage rites are performed and the couple engage in their first act of sexual intercourse, they are thereby married to each other indissolubly.[3] This would be a physicalistic view of human union and supposedly at its deepest. This would, in effect, make the juxtaposition of bodies *the* essential constituent of marriage. Mustn't consummation really be a deeper and richer reality than that? Doesn't human union in this case mean the becoming of one flesh for husband and wife—which in turn means total union, a union of both flesh and soul (*una caro, unio animorum*)? Are we to believe that this is automatically effected by the first intercourse after the wedding, or shouldn't we rather say that *when* consummation is achieved, and *whether* in fact it is achieved at all in any given case, is a matter of "mystery" (to use Marcel's term), a reality in which the couple themselves stand at the center of that which they examine?[4]

For this reason, some have suggested that the couple themselves, not marriage tribunals, decide about the reality or nonreality of their marriage. Whether the consequences of this position would lead in fact to the chaos of individual relativism is beside the point we are discussing here: namely, whether it is only the couple themselves who can decide the reality or nonreality of the mystery of their marriage, since it is they and only they who stand at the center of it. For other persons to make that decision would be to reduce it to the nature of a scientific matter, the sort of thing that can be judged objectively, from the outside looking in. And in a reality as intimately vital as marriage, such an approach seems inappropriate.

Thirdly, Mr. Antrobus' status of marriage to Mrs. Antrobus while he has his eyes on Sabina reminds one of the courtly love tradition of the Middle Ages, which looked on marriage as a *jurata fornicatio*, a pledged fornication.[5] This tradition held that man is by nature free in his attraction to women, and therefore adultery will always be in the offing as long as marriage is required by society. All great western literature, some have claimed, revolves on the theme of adultery.[6] Hence it was that Eleanor of Aquitaine's troubadours from southern France and the Minnesingers of Germany roamed through Europe in the Middle Ages singing of their ladies fair as always beyond the scope of a lasting earthly union. Only after death, and after many a sad pining brought forth in music, was consummation really to be hoped for. At a later day, Kierkegaard was to characterize this attitude as one in which a man loves Woman in general, any woman, but not this or that woman.[7] For this latter would entail commitment, a promise—in short, marriage. Put simply, the courtly love mentality took adultery as the great theme of human living, and the union of man and woman based on a promise of exclusivity and permanence as unnatural.

Well, what sort of reflections come to mind when confronted with such plain, no-nonsense talk about poor old human nature? I think, first of all, it would be silly to deny that a normal male (with apologies to Women's Lib) finds himself exercising a roving eye without much strenuous effort. And this whether he is married or not. Mixed with this play of the eyes between the sexes, as Arthur Schopenhauer (1788-1860) had already noted, is an element of flirtation in varying degrees: ". . . we see the glances of two lovers meet longingly; yet why so secretly, so fearfully and stealthily" etc.[8] I am afraid, though, that this is all somewhat beside the point we are discussing here, namely, the troubadourian view that married love is "boring" and a perversion of human love. Isn't there an increasing depth and quality of relationship in a genuine marriage which is a joy not gotten by flitting from flower to flower, so to speak? My surmise is that the troubadours simply romanticized their own experiences, since they were never known to be hesitant about taking a tumble with the village lass in the picturesque countrysides of southern France, while singing all the while of pure love, the pains of its vassalage, and—ah, its unattainability!

It appears, at any rate, that all these various views at least converge toward the point that marriage in essence is something other than merely the promise, something deeper; namely, human love. On the other hand, it seems equally foolhardy to me to go from a rigoristic view of permanence to the other extreme of discarding marriage altogether, thereby reducing human unions to a level unworthy of beings who are able to perceive the dynamism of their "meaningful relationship" precisely as moving toward permanence. We have seen how Freud himself, certainly not a believer in any intrinsic moral values, called the wish to do away with the family as an "indestructible feature of human nature" an *illusion* (see note 12, Chapter IV). In other words, isn't it natural to wish that a meaningful relationship will last? To say that a lasting and growing union between two persons is a perversion of human love when (or because) it is formalized into a permanent bond by a promise, seems to presuppose that promises and bonds are destructive of human relationships. Can any of us grow toward fullness without some sort of predictable behavior on the part of others, who constitute the environment in which our growth takes place? This is the all-important contribution promises and commitments make; namely, the setting up of a climate conducive to human efforts to move from fragment toward completion. One enters freely into a promise because he sees this as that which, in the long run, will enable him to exercise his freedom to the utmost. Similarly, one undertakes the marriage promise or vow in order to assure a pattern of behavior that will enable the couple to grow and develop in their love.

As for marriage ceremonies, they are obviously relative to the cultural practices of a group. Hence all the talk of "trial" marriages today may in fact be a very superficial expression of what is actually happening. The young, for instance, are not all that secretive—especially among themselves—as to which of them live together without benefit of judge or clergy. It is at least arguable that, amidst the cultural upheavals we are now undergoing, exposure of status to one's peers may be the equivalent of a rite of public promise, at least in those unions which in fact last.

Any discussion of the wholing process in married love cannot prescind from reflections on the role of sexual intercourse in human love. If the significance of the wedding ceremony is relativized, one can ask why sex should be regarded as right after the ceremony but wrong before it. In the understanding of marriage we are attempting to reach, the promise has a much less central place. It does not create a reality, that much is clear; it merely *conduces* toward the reality of union and continued growth by means of a public commitment to build love's wholeness continuously with the other. So what is there to bar the use of sex simply for experience, for the expression of affection no matter how temporary? Or, to put it more colloquially, what about the attitude that considers sex "no big thing"?

First of all, it is foolish, even dangerous, to hold that the sex act can be engaged in without entailing all sorts of emotional and spiritual involvements. Even the much heralded "liberation" or "revolution" brought about by the advent of the pill doesn't reduce the natural significance of the sex act as the *height* of a meaningful relationship between man and woman, in a very rich sense a *climax*, and not an experimental starting point for discovering whether such a meaningful relationship will "take" or not. What is a meaningful relationship anyway, if not mutual self-giving? Sex is in the picture because the giving of self among humans is an enfleshed intention, a real mingling of man's spirit and matter. St. Teresa's "divine love" as portrayed by Bernini[9] in Rome's Santa Maria della Vittoria is a vivid dramatization of the point: a languishing swoon with half-closed eyes and parted lips, a pose so graphically orgiastic that one wag supposedly commented, "If that is divine love, I know what it is!" In any man-woman relationship, the process of self-giving intensifies from physical exchanges of fondness up through a natural enchainment to the act of intercourse, paradoxically the most spiritual and at the same time most sensual expression of self-giving between persons. Intercourse, as a culminating point of reiterated self-giving, thus ties in with the view of tendential being we discussed earlier.

The point here is simply that intercourse can only be truly meaningful when it unifies the preceding and forthcoming sacrifices of the persons concerned, unifies them into a meaning the man and woman then stress to each other physically in coition. Engaged in without such preceding acts, without expectation of future acts, intercourse is an empty experience.[10] Engaged in out of sheer selfishness rather than self-giving, it is even destructive; it alienates and fragments rather than conduces toward wholeness, since it then most thoroughly reduces the other to the status of object. In other words, the ordinary experience of love is one of growing toward wholeness only through long, extended, and sustained self-giving. Thus, far from rendering lovemaking in a mature marriage stale (as the courtly lover thought), the growing unity and coordination in other phases of life redounds to the intensification of pleasure in the marriage act. Hence, a woman author writes:

> What is marriage? Sex! Sex in a way I had not understood or appreciated. To me sex is word, thought, affections, friendship and desire all knitted together. It is marriage, it is comfort and peace.[11]

Even if we grant that the pill may indeed have liberated women today from an earlier view of sex, it is still hard to get around the fact that it is the woman who "pays" whenever reversals in "meaningful relationships" occur. For that reason, the Anglican bishop of Woolwich in England in his pamphlet *Christian Morals Today*,[12] meant to calm troubled waters after his book *Honest to God*, argues movingly from the film *Room at the Top* that, while one may not absolutize morally on premarital sex, true concern for the other points to marriage as the right context for sexual union. Even more pointedly does Bertocci argue this matter in his book *Sex, Love, and the Person*. He shows how impossible it is to support by experience the so-called *Playboy* philosophy that the sex act can readily be engaged in without entailing all sorts of emotional and spiritual involvements. He asks:

> Do you love each other enough to forego what might indeed be the very meaningful experience of sexual union for the sake of creating the best conditions for its continued creativity in your lives.[13]

He wonders how long an unmarried couple can "continue to keep the experience high in quality, growing in quality, a binding force between them if, unmarried, they are not sharing the other investments of their lives." Someone may argue that they are indeed sharing all that, but if we suppose that to be really the case, then we are back to the question of marriage rites or ceremonies as relative. The point, at any rate, is that the human enterprise between a man and woman in love enough to marry consists precisely in the growth and enrichment of each other's lives through mutually held patterns of human values, always creatively attentive to the needs of the other as a growing person.

Enough has been said at this point, I think, to locate the role of sexual union within the process of growing wholeness between man and woman, that wholing process which we are in fact taking to be the very essence of marriage. What remains to be shown is just exactly how this reality and the marriage promise itself are related.

Let us concede outright that no man indeed knows his future; to this extent, surely, every promise is rooted in an impermanent state of mind. All one can do is one's best—this is true. But there is a hidden equivocation in that phrase, "do one's best." If one interprets it statically, as though one's best or utmost is a certain fixed amount of effort and no more, then indeed it is fraught with all sorts of disasters ready to descend on anyone entering the rocky path of living with another human being constantly. The interpretation, rather, should be that of a living and ongoing process, which strains to surpass the actual limits of any given moment as long as life lasts.

John Dewey is known for his opinion that all we can ever have in the human condition are merely ends-in-view, not ultimate ends-in-themselves.[14] What we are saying here is that "doing one's best" goes beyond the mere ends-in-view from stage to stage in our lives, goes beyond them to an overarching end-in-itself of one's life taken as a qualitative whole. I motivate the entire process of my life, in other words, by an attitude of mind—namely, creative faithfulness—in which my freedom deploys all my powers precisely toward upholding the commitment and promise I made to another person. The weakness of the earlier view of marriage we considered was its stress on the *promise* as the essence of marriage, even to the point where people could still be said to be married to each other after love had gone, perhaps even when hate had taken over, or when the "married" partners had gone their separate ways and built other wholes successfully.

What then is the essence of the wholing process we call marriage? Recall Toner's idea of radical love as a mutually-affirming affective presence of lover and beloved in each other precisely as actual persons, and not because of any other qualities or advantages that may accrue from the relationship. This radical love for each other is the ground and cause of mutual concern for each other. It is radical love we point to when, in attempting to answer the question why we feel concern for the other, we reply, "Because I love her." If pressed further as to the reason why we love her, we can only point to her and repeat the statement.

In recalling one's actual marriage, it seems clear that the essence of the event was this unique presential union, the free giving of selves to each other—exclusively and permanently—between man and woman, the building of a whole between them. The interesting thing is that this process of whole-building between the partners in marriage had surely already been taking place long before the day of the ceremony. How else could the couple's love have grown to the point where they now are to be "married," if there had been no self-giving before that time?

From the first moment of attraction, through the dating period and engagement, the process of self-giving in fact became a crescendo. Nor is there any stop, pause, or break in this process of self-giving *just before* the marriage vows and another discrete process of self-giving started *after* the promise. The reality in question here is simply *growing love*, continuous with itself before and after the promise. For before the promise this love between the engaged was already in fact the same exclusive and permanent love it is and continues to be in successful marriages. The promise, in short, merely ratified and proclaimed the reality that was there, the whole-building process going on within these two persons.

Nothing we have said here is inconsistent with the view that one should marry wholeheartedly and single-mindedly "for keeps." Especially when energized by a sacramental outlook, as in the Catholic tradition, such a view seems to combine within itself the ideal formula for a successful marriage. On the other hand, though, it seems only honest to call "marriages" that have gone to ruin by their proper names. To be consistent with our position on "telling it like it is," let us not say that growing love is present when it is *not*. For how is this sort of communication ever going to cultivate the admirable in the other?

The wholing of marriage is certainly a lifetime task, demanding the exertion always of more and more effort in creative fidelity to "do one's best" without limit while life lasts. This is the reality of growing love between man and woman that a public ritual first formalizes, establishing thereby the climate for that deep unity of persons which is the only reality that can properly be called "consummation." Indissolubility and permanence in marriage lie in the depth and intensity of this consummation, something that includes reflective terror at the thought it could ever end. Let us recall Dante's phrase: I-in-me-you and I-in-you-me *consummately*, to the point where in the wholing process of life one can say what Catherine says of Heathcliff in *Wuthering Heights*:

> If all else perished and he remained, I should still continue to be; and if all else remained and he were annihilated, the universe would turn into a mighty stranger. Nelly, I am Heathcliff! He's always, always, in my mind, not as a pleasure, any more than I am always a pleasure to myself, but as my own being. So don't talk of separation again.[15]

We are not, of course, advocating the context in which those words were said, since they were uttered in a situation more like courtly love than marriage. Our only point is that when, in marriage, unity and indissolubility and permanence are proposed as necessities, we should be clear that their reality is on the existential plane. Love, in other words, intensifies to the point of indissolubility and permanence when neither party would even wish to think or talk of separating.

This is the wholing process of man the fragment at its richest and deepest. And it is safe to say that it is ordinarily from this closest of human friendships that one then opens out to the ever-widening relationships of other wholes—children, neighbors, professional colleagues, and so forth—where growth takes place, as we have suggested, through the overlapping of intentionalities and through mediators.

COSMIC MEMORY AND BEYOND

Life is all about the wholing of self, my self. This is what we've been saying all along, and a reactive interpretation to the statement as though somehow it meant crass egoism would now be out of place. For we have stressed that wholing is synonymous with love, the tearing of myself out of myself as the center of all my living, toward what is *beyond* me. What is ever beyond is the whole, that whole I am building through my particular action here and now. This losing of self in the whole, as the self's only path to its own true being, constitutes the paradox and mystery of human life. It seems impossible to give a comprehensive account of why this is so; yet we know that self-centeredness, the "absolutizing of the fragment" in Marcel's words, is doomed to failure as a policy of human living. To repeat:

> If the self becomes entirely self-centered, a monstrous egoism follows, but as the self is now living on its own conceit and without external nourishment, the inflation is followed by collapse, a period of melancholia and death.[1]

Since this has been our theme, it may help to go back once more to the analogy of part and whole, to the example we used of the arm raising itself to ward off a fatal blow. In that one gesture is embodied the paradoxical mingling of self-recovery through self-loss. Were the arm so self-centered as to be unconcerned about the whole, it would not offer itself as the sacrifice —yet that would be the quickest path to self-destruction, that delusion of preserving itself through withdrawal from the descending blow and into itself. No hope, no life remains for the arm with the death of the man. Pressing this analogy further, we say that at no time must any one part fail to look beyond itself toward the whole man, aiming its acts always to the good of the whole.

Of course it can be objected that our example in fact illustrates the impossibility of ever veering away from self-centeredness, for the arm in effect loops its motive back to its own preservation in warding off the blow. There are at least three replies to such an objection. First, it is much too arbitrary an assumption to insist that someone is simply being self-centered at the very time his predominant impulse leads to acts of self-sacrifice. We have actual cases of soldiers hugging exploding grenades to themselves in order to save their buddies.[2] I suppose someone could still argue that this is still somehow selfish at bottom. But this would be like a Platonist who tells a fellow who swears he knew he was doing wrong and still did it, that surely the fellow didn't know that, or else he would never have done what he did! Or like Descartes' reply to the man who told the great philosopher that he really did not experience thinking at all in his sleep: Descartes countered that surely the fellow must be wrong, since he was still a man when he slept and the essence of man is to be a "thinking being"!

In plain words, there is incorrigible dogmatism in the objection. For what empirical evidences to the contrary will the objector accept as proof that there is indeed unselfishness in men? He is determined to force whatever evidences are put forward into a context of selfishness, like that legendary highwayman Procrustes who tied his victims upon his bed and stretched or cut off their legs to adapt them to its length. Since this is a point, however, that goes deep into our view of man's goodness or lack of it, perhaps we had better probe this common statement about human selfishness a bit further.

It is fair, I think, to ask anyone who insists that every man is "selfish" to clarify just what that word means to him. Does he mean it, for instance, in the same way one says that all humans move, digest, have two nostrils, etc.? In that case, he ought to admit he is not really saying anything significant. Yet, the way the statement is usually made indicates the speaker thinks he is making a distinctive point. We should therefore press him and ask: "What would one have to do for you to admit he is unselfish?" If no significant description is forthcoming, then we can only conclude that the word "unselfish" is really meaningless, and so too the original statement that all men are "selfish." Possibly we shouldn't have lingered so long on this point, except that it seems to matter greatly when it comes to admiring goodness in others and perhaps even emulating it. For we do have actual instances where a man volunteers to die in place of a condemned hostage who is a stranger, and it does not seem to make sense to downgrade such high moments of human goodness. Do we not all wish that such instances of nobility might even occur less rarely? And how is the dogmatic assertion that all men are "selfish" consistent with that wish?

Looking at the matter positively, we can also recall the nature of love as communion; namely, the mutual in-presence of the lovers in one another. In cases where the members of the wholing process are near and personal enough to be in radical love with one another, it is fallacious to talk of looping one's motive back to oneself, since the other whom I love contains me and I him, as we saw in our earlier sections on Marcel and Toner. We have to be careful to admit, however, that the "whole" we have been talking about is only analogous to such *objective* wholes as finished houses or something brought to completion from a blueprint. The word "whole" is said of objects and of human subjects in partly the same yet altogether different meanings. A human whole is partly the same in that more than one component part goes into composing what is larger than any of the individual parts themselves. But it is totally different in that there never is a time in human wholes when I can say, as I can and do say about objective blueprints, that this or that thing is now finished or completed. For as we saw in the preceding chapter on marriage, fidelity is not static, involving so much effort and no more—an attitude that would tend toward destruction rather than construction of human wholes. Thus whether we take Camus' notion of *rebellion* against the absurd in life,[3] or whether we take the dynamic view of life as tendential, a meaningful life would in both cases be seen as transcending the bounds of its own self at any given moment. The wholes it moves toward look always beyond what the self is at any moment. To insist that this is simply egoism after all is surely nothing but incorrigible dogmatism.

Why then use the analogous word "whole" at all in what seems to be a completely diverse area where completion is never reached? Once more we fall back on the insight that the individual is merely a part or fragment whose path toward fullness is through constructive interpersonal relationships, the access points to others being language, the face, and virtuous mediation. That impulse in the human fragment toward transcendence with others, therefore, leads the mind to read the goal of that impulse as the positive correlative of *part*, namely, the *whole*. And this is the basis for analogy. Moreover, the idea of human life as wholing passes the test of any good insight; namely, its power to organize other significant ideas and experiences around itself as a living center. Let's examine at least one instance of this in the realm of ethics.

We have seen how the view of life as wholing leads to the question of what a man ought and ought not to do, surely a significant component of all human living. Now it is possible to make a case that the view of life as wholing enables one to assimilate both the absolute and relative characteristics of ethical considerations satisfactorily. For one would then view an immoral action as what is unwholesome, something that balances out on "total consideration" as destructive of harmonious human relations. Even if perhaps only rarely, such moral absolutes nevertheless can be reached. It seems impossible, for example, to ever see child-battering or rape as other than destructive, and so always unethical. One who forces himself to imagine fantastic situations in order to make either of those actions appear somehow constructive should see the implication of his intense effort: namely, the improbability of his own answer. And if he moves on to object that no mere man can ever consider the "total situation," we admit that in talking of the "total situation" here we don't mean a man must be more than a man; no, by *total* we mean precisely what he sees in exercising his human powers to the utmost upon available data. To require more is absurd; to require less bespeaks that insincerity of heart which Kierkegaard noted as the source of all immorality.

By "total consideration," then, we mean our human condition together with a sincere heart, the essential components of any moral act. To consider totally means to make a situational decision as to which whole, of the many wholes pressing their claims on me in my situation, has the claim on my action here and now.[4] This is the relative dimension of morality that must be worked out individually and situationally. Yet though relative, a definitive judgment is nevertheless possible as to the badness of an act that "constructs" the wrong whole at the wrong time. Time is truly of the essence in morals, and an untimely "constructive" act is a contradiction in terms.

Does this force us back, then, to an infinite regress on the question of right timing? The human mind, in its cunning, can conjure all sorts of rationalizations to defend our actions as always the right and "constructive" ones. That is why we have presented approvingly a notion of love as wholing which implies both mind and heart, both faith and sincerity before

God and myself. There is no escape into infinite regress when God the Absolute and Ultimate Being confronts me in my ethical decision. Nor is there any escape in the other direction, beyond myself, who, by my reflective powers of willing and thinking, stand present to myself and my actions simultaneously. Bonhoeffer puts this well in one of his own attempts to view morality as at once ultimate yet situational, absolute yet relative.

> An ethic cannot be a book in which there is set out how everything in the world ought to be but unfortunately is not. . . . The essential character of free responsibility makes it impossible to establish laws defining when and to what extent such a departure from the "limited field of accomplishments" forms part of a man's calling and of his responsibility towards men. Such a departure can be undertaken only after a serious weighing up of the vocational duty which is directly given, of the dangers of interference in the responsibility of others, and finally of the totality of the question which is involved.[5]

But can the idea of human wholing hold together against what seems to be a weakness at its center: namely, its entailment of essential incompletion? If one is forever transcending oneself toward various wholes, then those wholes, themselves human, surely share the same characteristic of transcendence. Isn't this Sisyphus and his boulder all over again?

How have we thought our way beyond Sisyphus if, whether in the immediacy of the individual or in the ultimacy of the wholes, the *beyond* is nothing more than a tantalizing constant? Beyond what—that is to say, our point of departure as the individual fragment—is clear. But *toward what* is the question. Is there nothing, not even cosmic memory (as we saw one writer phrase it),[6] that in some way preserves our life's strivings?

Let us treat the question as it is posed, on the level of immediacy and also of ultimacy: the level of daily living, and the level of preserving all that has gone into a meaningful life, through God and immortality.

1 IMMEDIACY

We have already noted the analogous character of the word "whole" when applied to both objects and free human subjects. All we need to do here is show a possible way of making sense out of the word "whole" when applied to the immediacy of life's events, even though these events themselves, as we admit, are always moving on *beyond* themselves to something else. "Once I turn in upon my finished work and become engrossed in it . . . it is transformed into a having, something clutched in a dead hand," we recall Marcel saying.[7] Is not this a reduction of the self to pure becoming?

We have attempted previously to hold being and becoming within the self. Do the necessarily shifting components of our human wholes invalidate or make less authentic the process of wholing simply because they shift? It is natural, for example, for children at some time to go forth and start their own family wholes. Yet does that in any way take back the process of wholing the parents engaged in while the children were children and contained within the parental whole? Why should it, if what we have proposed all along is true: that *the only path to human wholing is expending oneself for the whole, relative to situational time and place?* Shifts because of circumstances, fate, choice, or whatever, are thus secondary and supportive of the self's wholing process. What is primary, what is basic and most authentic to the process of wholing, is that the self be for the whole at any given moment.

In a sense, even the terrible interruption of death loses its sting when it comes to a man who is correctly situated in the task of building wholes. Isn't the substance of any man's life, in other words, to be doing the right thing? Because of the infinity in the self, an idea we saw in Kierkegaard, the *whole* is always beyond and more than what he has, at any time, achieved. What is important is to make of one's life a continual wholing process.

2 ULTIMACY

If death is the absolutely final limit, the total extinction of
everything human effort and living have achieved, how does
one view the meaning of life? This raises the question of immortality and God, a question that may be considered in two
antithetical ways. One either looks at the matter *discontinuously*—i.e., there is no immortality and no God (or if there is,
this has nothing to do with what is going on in my life)—or else
one adopts the rationalistic standpoint of viewing everything
in life as a preparation for the state *after* death, in unveiled
relationship with God. We already discussed this second position, when we presented the here and the hereafter as necessarily continuous within the context of the meaning of one's
life.[8] Before sorting out some middle way, however, we shall
have to examine the position that dismisses immortality and
God out of hand, and savors only life's experiences solely
within their own caducal context. We find a good expression of
this position in Simone de Beauvoir's book, *The Ethics of Ambiguity*, where she writes:

> Man, mankind, the universe and history are, in Sartre's expression
> "detotalized totalities," that is, separation does not exclude relation,
> nor vice versa. It is not true that the mind has to choose between the
> contingent absurdity of the discontinuous and the rationalistic neces-
> sity of the continuous; on the contrary, it is part of its function to
> make a multiplicity of coherent ensembles stand out against the
> unique background of the world, and inversely, to comprehend these
> ensembles in the perspectives of an ideal unity of the world.[9]

Here is a view that rejects immortality and God, and then proceeds from this "detotalization" to rear up a totality of life's
experiences, of human adventures against "the background of
time, each finite to each, though they are all open to the infinity of the future." There are many things to be said, certainly, in favor of this view of life's meaning, though it is
impossible here to go into them all. Suffice it to say that it may
intensify the tang of living, of savoring every moment of life,

to realize the sure imminence and finality of death. It seems difficult to fault the view that "if we do not love life on our own account, and through others, it is futile to seek to justify it in any other way."[10]

Simone de Beauvoir (1908–) points out, for instance, that the ensemble of events leading to the liberation of Paris during World War II "were an immense collective festival exalting the happy and absolute end of that particular history which was precisely the occupation of Paris."[11] It was just bad faith on the part of those who demurred about all the wild jubilation, on the score that soon life, liberated life, would have its own set of problems.[12] The very meaning of a festival is the absolute termination of some particular evil that has been wiped off the face of the earth, and there is a deep impulse within those who have worked against that evil to preserve, to absolutize, that moment of joy which they realize only too well cannot last. This yearning to hold forever the moment of triumphant joy is symbolized, for example, in the smashing of wine goblets after the last of the wine has been drained in a festival—that joy which everyone knows will pass away all too soon, never to return.[13] The festival is indeed man's counterposture against the transitoriness of life's adventures, whose iron law will inevitably bring the joyous moment down. In other words, it is precisely a sense of "ratio and measure" in the mixed condition of life (Dewey's words in our earlier chapter) that calls sometimes for total celebration when struggles for a human good succeed.

Simone de Beauvoir also notes the ambiguity of meaning in the word "end": namely, end as goal or end as fulfillment.[14] The goal of one's strivings may orient itself beyond the individual to the totality of time and the human species, but this is beside the point as far as the individual's meaningful striving in life is concerned. The individual can take the moment of fulfillment, the festival, as an absolute, even as he realizes the larger horizon of time and future men "each finite to each,"

that may be the goal of his own efforts. In an existence con-
sciously discontinuous with God and immortality, then, we find
a view that seems to combine the absolute and the relative
within a finite this-worldly perspective, even to the point of
coupling again, those twins we met earlier, love and death.

> The king is dead, long live the king! Thus the present must die so
> that it may live; existence must not deny this death which it carries
> in its heart; it must assert itself as an absolute in its very finiteness. It
> is obvious that this finiteness is not that of the pure instinct; we have
> said that the future was the meaning and the substance of all action,
> . . . but maintain that one must not expect that this goal be justified
> as a point of departure of a new future; insofar as we no longer have
> a hold on the time which will flow beyond its coming, we must not
> expect anything of that time for which we have worked; other men
> will have to live its joys and sorrows. The tasks which we have set
> up for ourselves and which, through exceeding the limits of our lives,
> are ours, must find their meaning in themselves, and not in a mythical
> historical end.[15]

What can one say about this powerful position? As with
everything else, for those completely persuaded of it there is of
course nothing more to be said. For those who may not be so
sure, however, it may help to recall Hartshorne's words, quoted
earlier in Chapter I:

> It is useless to say the better is better as long as you are alive. For
> when you and the rest are nothing, there is then no better and no
> worse for your sojourn, if the universe also forgets. To suppose other-
> wise is merely an illicit fancy that there is after all a cosmic memory,
> which is a partial reintroduction of a God into the world.[16]

Is not Simone de Beauvoir trying to forge a position here of
"absolutizing the moment" at the same time that she carefully
manages to keep an opening toward *infinity*, even if this be
within her own version of it? One would have to reflect hon-
estly on whether there is not in her position a drive toward
something that will remain of one's absolutized festive moments beyond the moment of their fall. She herself says many

things that seem to lead beyond the position she explicitly advocates. She writes, for instance:

> Thus we have an example how man must assume his finiteness; not by treating his existence as transitory or relative but by reflecting the infinite within it; by treating it as an absolute.[17]

Again, she has a sentence in that same locus which can serve nicely as a transition toward the positive part of this chapter on immortality and God. She writes:

> There is liberation of man only if, in aiming at itself, freedom is achieved absolutely in the very fact of aiming at itself.[18]

This is our point of parting from Simone de Beauvoir's notion of transcendence within a finite self-enclosed world. For a limited being that shows its peculiar power of complete self-reflection, as in freedom aiming at itself, shows intimations of immortality. This very same observation can be made of Kurt Vonnegut's statement about pretender and pretension in man, which we quoted earlier. The pretender is simultaneously able to contain within himself his pretension, and to know both by the single act of consciousness he employs at the time he knows both. We are agreeing with Simone de Beauvoir, in other words, and yet drawing a far different conclusion from the notion of freedom aiming at itself and thereby achieving the absolute.

Behind this thought is the unspoken premise that a limited being, by knowing its limit precisely as a limit, thereby transcends that limit. It is a thought often enough expressed among philosophers—Georg Hegel (1770-1831), Henri Bergson (1859-1941), and Ludwig Wittgenstein (1889-1951), for instance—[19] and though we touched on this point earlier, it may help to linger on it one last time. If I am truly ignorant of something, for example, I am enclosed by this particular limitation. There is no way out of such an enclosure, and it makes no sense to say that I somehow transcend that ignorance if I am not even aware of my ignorance. But it is an entirely different matter, once I realize my ignorance and my limitation; at that moment of realization, I am already a step outside of my ignorance toward knowledge, and thus outside the limit. This principle certainly seems to be a sound one.

Now, as we saw from the start, the problem of the self arises precisely because of the presence in man of the power of reflection—the ability to look at himself, point to himself in his entirety, to be asker and asked at one and the same time. Is this not a clear instance of man knowing his limits and thus transcending those limits of his?

Now it seems impossible to assign such a power to any bodily organ, for none of our bodily organs are able to go beyond themselves or beyond the context of the concrete object that stimulates them at the moment. In other words, organic perceptions themselves are not perceptive of themselves in one and the same act by which they perceive their objects. The eye does not see itself in one and the same act in which it sees this or that colored object. The tongue does not taste itself in one and the same act by which it tastes this or that flavored thing. Therefore we say those organs are completely within the scope of their environmental objects.

This is not true, however, of the reflective power of consciousness, which enables man to watch and point to himself in his entirety. And it should be stressed that we point to ourselves in our entirety—not to that one part of my chest, for instance, over which the tip of my forefinger may be resting. *I* point to the entire *me*. Thus we see how man can be both pretender and pretended, asker and asked, and able even to will that the limitation of the human will itself be surpassed, or absolutized, as we have been saying. What then should we say of death, which is man's supposedly final limit, yet a limit of which he is fully aware?

The finest lines in human literature are many of them musings on death. To cite only one example, Tolstoy's *The Death of Ivan Ilyich* shows human consciousness not only meditating, thinking, on death, but doing far more. In it we watch a man resisting death's advance with all his might. In the end, physically spent but spiritually transformed, we see him bow down to welcome the irresistible. Men are so intrigued by death, in fact, that university seminars have been established to study how the dying think about dying. Elisabeth Kübler-Ross' book *On Death and Dying* is a good example.[20] In it we can observe dying men reflecting on themselves to the very end. Invariably, those among them who resented their terminal condition echo the point we made in an earlier chapter. It is not death that pains them so much in their last days, but its *untimeliness*; those whom they love and with whom their lives were wholed still need them so much. There can be no doubt about their profound awareness of their own death and its implications. It is difficult to imagine anyone reading such a book of detailed interviews recorded by the dying without being affected somehow. And if one is affected at all, it will most probably take some form or other of a reflection on his own death as well. To conclude these illustrations, we can perhaps point up the decisive difference in quality between reflective human consciousness and subhuman consciousness by recalling instances of one of the most brutal of all humanities. I refer to those war atrocities in which prisoners were ordered to dig their own graves before their clearly impending execution— a horror surely peculiar to humans, since it attacks life at its intensest point: reflective consciousness.

Our question again is this: If I think about my own death, reflect on it, meditate on it, and so forth, can I still say I am completely within its power? Am I contained by death as my absolute limit when I reflect on that very limit itself?[21] If so, what of the premise that to know a limit is already to be beyond that limit itself? It should be clear then that the position preferred here (granting all the while the power and attraction of a completely this-worldly position such as that of Simone de Beauvoir), is that the process of wholing does not stop but propels itself beyond death. Should someone object that by this logic only those truly reflective persons who see the limit of death and reflect on it are immortal, I would have to agree that not every man indeed thinks on death in the manner we have implied above and it does seem much easier to hold that only those are immortal who face death fearlessly, especially for a principle or a conviction they uphold, in contrast to the craven and cowardly spirits who, as Shakespeare well noted, die a thousand times over. Why not say, then, that only those are immortal who show themselves superb of will and intellect in the lives they lead? The difficulty with conceding this point is that it would change those "great spirits" into something other than human beings. If they are great, they are great in the context of human endeavor and achievement; they are great *human* beings. And this is to say that they belong, all the same, to the same species of being as do their lesser fellows. Even these lesser men, after all, are *able* to recognize their ignorance, to think about their own deaths, to admire the great ones and wish in their own way they could be like them, etc. What are all these if not variations on the theme of realizing one's own limits, and thereby being beyond those limits?

The difference stated in the objection, in other words, is not one of kind, but of degree. It is not a difference based on the absence or presence of the power of reflection, but on the depth and intensity of its use. So there is nothing in all we have said to prevent the conclusion that immortal life probably differs in intensity from individual to individual, depending on the power of the self to transcend its own death through reflective thinking and willing.

Nor would disbelief in God and immortality make the meaning of life that we have presented invalid. For is there not the same propulsion from fragment toward the whole, and beyond that toward totality of some sort, even in a sheer humanism such as that of Simone de Beauvoir? Is not that propulsion toward totality, no matter how "each finite to each," an indication of belief in some sort of cosmic memory? Between the believer and nonbeliever at this point stands only the differentiating belief or nonbelief in the self either continuing on or not continuing beyond death toward completion. The nonbeliever constructs a view of totality within an absolutely material context; it is in this context for him that the wholing process is situated. The believer views all the wholing processes going on in the material universe as centered in God, toward whom all creatures tend as their ground and center. In St. Thomas' words:

> It is clear that God is the common good of the whole universe and of all its parts. Thus a created being in its own way naturally loves God more than itself; beings without consciousness do this simply by their natural operations, animals by their acts of sense consciousness, and rational beings through intellectual love.[22]

But whether one believes or not, what emerges finally as the most important point of all is not so much the *having* of wholes which I have helped build, but the being *I become* in my wholing efforts sustained through a lifetime.

Is this not a terribly empty conclusion to reach after so long a road: namely, that death comes when it does come to each one of us keeping at the process of becoming whole yet never quite making it? To raise this question is to have missed the essential import of love as a wholing process, the one theme we traced in all the preceding pages. The wholing process of love *wholes* by entering the individual's fragmented condition and making present in him the beings of all those he loves. If all those he loves are *in* him, then not only they but all those present in them as well are likewise in the individual whose fragmentation was transcended. This point we brought out in our earlier chapter on the infinity of the face. Furthermore, we should look at the other side of the wholing process. I not only take others into me; I am myself taken into others. The wholing process takes one out of his fragmentation insofar as he is loved by others and thereby *in them* through the communion of love, as we saw in our section on Toner and in our reflections on marriage. For instance, my wife loves me and my children. Do I not "repeat," refind myself, my children, her friends in her? This is why cosmic memory of some sort is built into the wholing process. We can recall St. Augustine's words, quoted earlier, about his decision to continue living, if only to make sure that his friend who had just died might continue to live on in him and not perish altogether.

It is clear then how we can say the wholing process is never positively completed this side of death. So long as a man is alive, he is always open to the possibility of befriending a stranger, and even more important, to the possibility of being loved by any stranger at all who may chance to see his face. This positive opening toward an infinity was precisely what brought us to our final question of limiting or not limiting the context of friendship exclusively to the confines of human mortality. In Simone de Beauvoir we saw an illustration of one who answers yes to this question. And there are those of us who, with Gabriel Marcel, look on this profound longing for eternal endurance of this most beautiful of all human achievements, *friendship*—and believe that the reality which surrounds us and which we participate is a Person, sympathetic to our faith and our longings, and who joins us as we face those we love and say: You shall not die![23]

NOTES

PREFACE

1 F. Ç. Kolbe, *A Catholic View of Holism*, p. vi.
2 For an introductory bibliography on Aquinas' metaphysics of existence, see Domingo Báñez, *The Primacy of Existence in Thomas Aquinas*, translated by Benjamin S. Llamzon. I may mention here that although Abraham Maslow in his book, *Toward a Psychology of Being*, advocates a holistic view of man, his concept of the self as an "embryonic potential" (p. 160 and passim) is so alien to my own understanding of potentiality as a metaphysical term that I have prescinded from it, in spite of Maslow's explicit step from psychology to philosophy.
3 Henry D. Thoreau, *Walden*, p. 17. My quote from Thoreau in the epigraph is from p. 81. In his book, *The Conditions of Philosophy*, Mortimer J. Adler also makes this point through his distinction between "second order" questions regarding textual subtleties, etc., in the statements and writings of philosophers and "first order" questions which philosophize directly on life problems and situations. Adler's full title contains an intriguing comment about philosophy: *Its Checkered Past, Its Present Disorder, and Its Future Promise*. See also note 14, Chapter I below. And hundreds of years ago, at a climacteric in the history of science, Galileo Galilei (1564-1642) wrote: "A man will never become a philosopher by worrying forever about the writings of other men, without ever raising his own eyes to nature's works" ("The Assayer," in *Discoveries and Opinions of Galileo*, p. 225). And again, "Perhaps Sarsi believes that all the host of good philosophers may be enclosed within four walls. I believe that they fly, and that they fly alone, like eagles, and not in flocks like starlings. It is true that because eagles are rare birds they are little seen and less heard, while birds that fly like starlings fill the sky with shrieks and cries, and wherever they settle befoul the earth beneath them" (Ibid., p. 230).

CHAPTER I

1 Kurt Vonnegut, *Mother Night*, p. 160.

2 See Ernest Jones, *The Life and Work of Sigmund Freud*, vol. 1, p. 306; vol. 2, p. 413; also note 17, Chapter V below. See also Sigmund Freud, *Collected Papers*, vol. 4, p. 317. Freud believed a man owes nature one life, in the sense (it seems) of letting nature take its course in this matter. For despite his terrible years of suffering and wasting away, to the point where even his favorite dog recoiled from him during the last phase of his life, there is no account of his ever having raised the issue of suicide. *Höchst überflussig* ("most uncalled for") was all he would say of his condition. This is also confirmed by Max Schur, Freud's personal physician. Except for almost day-to-day medical diaries and some personal letters, however, Max Schur's book, *Freud: Living and Dying*, doesn't really improve on Jones' account. In fact much of Schur's book are bulky repetitions of what Jones and Freud himself already published elsewhere.

3 Immanuel Kant, *Critique of Judgment*, p. 353. See more of Kant's thought on this point in "Conjectural Beginning of Human History: Concluding Remarks," where he writes: "To be sure, a man who can wish that life should last longer than in fact it does must be a poor judge of its values. Its greater length would merely prolong a game of increasing war with troubles . . ." (*On History*, pp. 66-68). In "The End of All Things," he cites four allegories that show the earth successively as an inn, a penitentiary, a lunatic asylum, and a cloaca (Ibid., pp. 73-74). Still, with an optimism based on the French Revolution, Kant felt that all in all we can say that "the human race has always been in progress toward the better and will continue to be so henceforth" ("An Old Question Raised Again," in Ibid., pp. 147-48).

4 George Santayana, *Persons and Places*, vol. 1, p. 33. William James, interestingly enough, makes somewhat the same observations about some Boston society people: "Many Bostonians, *crede experto* (and inhabitants of other cities, too, I fear) would be happier men and women today if they could once for all abandon the notion of keeping up a Musical Self, and without shame let people hear them call a symphony a nuisance" (*Psychology*, p. 54). James is mocking here not the symphony, but the busywork which goes with pretending to be a lover of the symphony.

5 Santayana, *Persons and Places*, vol. 1, pp. 179-80. For an authentic account that throws light on the many apparent inconsistencies between Santayana's philosophy and personal life, see Daniel Cory, *Santayana: The Later Years*.

6 William James, *The Will To Believe*, p. 212.

7 Alfred N. Whitehead, *Science and the Modern World*, p. 51.

8 Charles Hartshorne, Review of *Science and the Idea of God* by William E. Hocking, *Philosophy of Phenomenological Research* 6:454, 1945-1946. I do not mean that one should go to the other extreme of philosophical dogmatism, especially on a matter such as we are grappling with in this book. A habit of suspending belief for purposes of purification is, after all, as old as philosophy itself, as Philip P. Hallie shows in *Scepticism, Man and God*.

9 Albert Camus, *The Myth of Sisyphus*, p. 38.

10 Ibid., p. 16.

11 Kurt Vonnegut, *Cat's Cradle*, p. 124.

12 Vonnegut, *Mother Night*, p. 178.

13 Vonnegut, *Cat's Cradle*, p. 164.

14 Camus, *Myth of Sisyphus*, p. 45. See Walter Kaufmann's criticism of Camus as a "fine writer, but not a philosopher" especially on this notion of revolt against the absurd, in *The Meaning of Death*, edited by Herman Feifel, pp. 54-60. Heidegger, too, on his idea of death, comes in for his share of Kaufmann's lampooning: "One read him, found him difficult, persevered, spent years studying him, and—what else could one do after years of study of that sort? One became a teacher of philosophy, protecting one's investment by 'explaining' Heidegger to students, warding off objections by some such remark as 'There is much that I, too, don't understand as yet, but I shall give my life trying to understand a little more'" (Ibid., p. 51). A more sympathetic reading of Heidegger on life situations and his similarities of thought to W. James may be found in William A. Sadler, *Existence and Love*, pp. 64-94.

15 John Dewey, *Experience and Nature*, p. 46.

16 Ibid., p. 41.

17 Ibid., p. 71. It is not as though the element of the absurd is something only modern man has perceived. The ancient Pythagoreans, who believed that everything was numbers, still knew about the impossibility of finding a common measure between the sides of a rectangle and their diagonal, though they kept this a professional secret. In the *Theaetetus*, we find the characters conversing about the "surd." See Francis M. Cornford, *Plato's Theory of Knowledge*, p. 23. As regards Dewey, the last impression I would wish to give by quoting him on this notion of "ratio, measure" in life is that he advocates resignation in life. On the contrary, Dewey's theme in all his writings is that of restlessly striving to improve on and do away with the "bads" of life through science and critical intelligence, resisting all the while the Greek penchant for fixing one's view of reality in ultimates.

18 Dietrich Bonhoeffer, *Letters and Papers from Prison*, p. 94.

19 Ibid., p. 164.

20 Ibid., p. 119.

CHAPTER II

1 The problem of the self is raised in various ways: Who am I? What am I? Is there an I? (See note 18, Chapter II below.) Or even, "if there is a problem of the self, its solution is that the self is a problem," the theme of Henry W. Johnstone, Jr.'s book, *The Problem of the Self*, p. xi. By this, Johnstone means that the self arises out of the person only in actually contradictory moments of consciousness, as exemplified in Zerlina's "*vorrei e non vorrei*" in Mozart's opera *Don Giovanni*. See Johnstone, *Problem of Self*, pp. 18, 29.

2 John S. Mill, *Three Essays on Religion*, in *Collected Works*, vol. 10, p. 388.

3 Henri Bergson says: "The moment there is any regard for us, even if the intention is not good, we begin to count for something in the universe. That is what experience tells us. But, even before we consult experience, it would seem highly unlikely that humanity should have begun by theoretical views of any sort or kind. We shall say it over and over again: before a man can philosophize, man must live" (*The Two Sources of Morality and Religion*, p. 176). The distinction here is between *esse* and *bene esse*, between barely existing and existing well. The search for meaning in life (philosophy) occurs when man has reached the level of existing well. Yet it is more complex than that; for if this search is unsuccessful, it can boomerang full force and destroy everything one has achieved toward existing well. To add more complexity, one recalls Viktor E. Frankl's well-known book, *Man's Search for Meaning*, which illustrates how meaning in life was the decisive factor in achieving just bare survival under the worst of conditions. Frankl was not observing the enactment of his theory among prisoners who were philosophizing; he elaborated the theory upon subsequent reflection, after he and all the rest had been liberated.

Paul Ricoeur, with delicate precision, shows how the Thomistic and Cartesian treatises on the passions are deficient because of their objectifying view of the "good," even when they supposedly distinguish this from the good qua human. Ricoeur thinks the Kantian trilogy of the passions, *habsucht, herrschsucht, ehrsucht* ("possession," "domination," "prestige"), points up the necessary intertwining of human passions with the cultural and economic spheres, where alone the goods of man are available. Within that cultural and economic context, we find human persons who are good-in-themselves, absolute worths—ends-in-themselves, in Kant's terms. This is the primal affirmation an individual must believe and make of himself and others, and those others of himself. Beyond this primal point, the desire for recognition, "the desire of desire," is extremely fraught with all sorts of aberrations, disorders, and even total tragedies. "The possibility of being no more than the word of another, the dependence on fragile opinion, these are precisely the occasion for the passions of glory which graft their vanity onto the fragility of esteem as opinion. This opining nature of esteem keeps the search for recognition within the median zone of affectivity, above the level of the will to live, and even above the feelings which cluster around having and power, but not within the sphere of Eros, which Plato said creates in beauty and in accordance with the body and soul. The mutual constitution of men in mutual esteem, as long as it remains opinion, is not yet within the sphere of that creation" (*Fallible Man*, pp. 184-85). See also Ricoeur's book, *Freud and Philosophy*, pp. 506-14.

4 Max Scheler, *The Nature of Sympathy*, p. 159.

5 David Hume, *A Treatise of Human Nature*, p. 423.

6 I do not refer to anything esoteric here, like the Freudian concept of the subconscious, or innate ideas, etc. I simply mean probing and analyzing presuppositions and implications entailed in one's view of things which have not been clarified and sorted out in one's mind. On the inaccessibility of the Freudian subconscious itself except through representations, see Ricoeur, *Freud and Philosophy*, pp. 134-51.

7 For Thomas Aquinas on *esse* as "subsisting, tending, and resting," see *De Veritate*, XXI, 2; also, *Summa Contra Gentiles*, Book III, where he shows how all beings are in dynamic tendency toward the supreme good. Here are a few illustrative texts:

"That toward which a thing tends, while it is without it, and wherein it rests when it has it, is its end. Now anything that is without its proper perfection is moved towards it, as far as in it lies; and if it have that perfection it rests therein" (*Contra Gentiles*, III, c. 16).

"Things tend to be like God insofar as he is good. Now it is out of his goodness that God bestows being on others, for all things act inasmuch as they are actually perfect. Therefore, all things seek to be like God in this respect by being causes of others" (Ibid., c. 22).

"Natural bodies, devoid of knowledge, tend to an end as directed thereto by an intelligent substance, in the same way as an arrow directed by the archer tends to the mark. . . . By tending to their own perfection, they tend to a good, since a thing is good insofar as it is perfect. And according as a thing tends to be good, it tends towards a divine likeness, since a thing is like God insofar as it is good" (Ibid., c. 24).

"It is manifest that God is the common good of the entire universe and of all its parts. Hence each creature in its own way loves God naturally more than itself. Beings without consciousness in their own natural motion, brute animals through their actions of sense consciousness, . . . but rational beings through an intellectual tendency which is called love" (*Quodlibetales*, 1, a. 8).

8 Plato, *The Republic*, Book VII. For Plato on knowledge, see Cornford, *Plato's Theory of Knowledge*, or Sir David Ross, *Plato's Theory of Ideas*.

9 *Symposium*, 212. On love in Plato, see Thomas Gould, *Platonic Love*, or Douglas N. Morgan, *Love: Plato, the Bible and Freud*, pp. 5-46.

10 *Nicomachean Ethics*, Books VIII and IX, in Aristotle, *Basic Works*, pp. 1058-93. On the absence in Plato and Aristotle of the equivalent to the modern term "will," see Vernon J. Bourke, *Will in Western Thought*, pp. 29-33, or Michael J. O'Brien, *The Socratic Paradoxes and the Greek Mind*, pp. 205-28.

11 *Nicomachean Ethics*, 1169a.

12 See note 7, Chapter II above.

13 *Summa Theologiae*, I, q. 82, a. 1, ad 3.

14 Ibid., q. 83, a. 1, c.

15 Meditation VI, in René Descartes, *Philosophical Works*, vol. 1, p. 195.

16 For the concept of nothingness as the very center and essence of human freedom, see Jean-Paul Sartre, *Being and Nothingness*, Part I, ch. 1, pp. 33-116, where Sartre presents man as a being who causes nothingness to arise in the world, since man himself is affected with nonbeing because he alone is *free*, able to withdraw and produce negations. See also Mary Schaldenbrand, "Freedom and the I: An Existential Inquiry," *International Philosophical Quarterly* 3:571-99, December 1963.

17 Immanuel Kant, *Fundamental Principles of the Metaphysics of Morals*, p. 11.

18 See Gerald E. Myers, *Self*. This book is rich with material on the question of the self. Myers follows Hume who wrote in his *Treatise of Human Nature*, ". . . when I enter most intimately into what I call *myself*, I always stumble on some particular perception or other. If anyone thinks he has a different notion of *himself* I must confess I can reason no longer with him." Thus Myers thinks the question "what am I?" is a philosophical "howler," unlike "who am I?" or "what sort of a person am I?" which are answerable. There are philosophers who reduce human consciousness to the nervous system entirely, and Myers rejects this position (pp. 39-41). But then he goes on to advocate the ultimacy of "naked thoughts" and is fascinated by Wittgenstein's remark that "we are all naked underneath our clothes." It seems to me that there is a failure here to see that "naked" is essentially reflective of the self that bonds memories, perceptions, and states or conditions precisely as mine *simultaneously*. (Of course, one can also reflect subsequently on those conditions, but that would be a different matter.) Otherwise, our reflexive remarks about ourselves would mean nothing at all, since we remember and make remarks about our memories only in the present! This same criticism can be made of James' functional identity theory that "the thoughts themselves are the thinkers" in *Psychology*, pp. 43-83. This whole controversy on objectifying our subjectivity once we look in on ourselves, since introspection is always retrospection, and so giving rise to what is called the "problem of the 'vanishing experience,'" all pivots on whether human consciousness is capable of knowing and knowing that it knows *in one and the same act*. On the question of whether there is an "I" at all, as in Indian philosophy, see Troy W. Organ's overpriced book, *The Self in Indian Philosophy*.

19 Thoreau's version of the medieval saying *corruptio optimi pessima* is masterful: "There is no odor so bad as that which arises from goodness tainted" (*Walden*, p. 66).

20 Again one can point to Martin Luther who had the most rigorous training in Catholicism as an institution, and yet one day rose up to repudiate that institution. For a psychoanalytic interpretation of Luther's *turmerlebnis* (his moment of illumination "on the privy in the tower") see Norman O. Brown, *Life Against Death*, p. 102.

21 Herbert Marcuse, *Eros and Civilization*, p. 12.

22 Peter Homans, *Theology after Freud*, p. 26. See also J. Preston Cole, *The Problematic Self in Kierkegaard and Freud*, pp. 33-54, 102-26, 175-96. (And see note 35, Chapter III below.)

23 James, *Will To Believe*, p. 277. G. W. F. Hegel has an intriguing idea about the human hand, though in an antiquated context, in his *The Phenomenology of Mind*: "That the hand, however, must exhibit and reveal the inherent nature of individuality as regards its fate is easily seen from the fact that, after the organ of speech, it is the hand most of all by which a man actualizes and manifests himself. It is the animated artificer of his fortune: we may say of the hand it is what a man does, for in it as the effective organ of self-fulfillment he is there present as the animating soul; and since he is ultimately and originally his own fate, the hand will express thus this innate inherent nature" (pp. 342-43).

24 "The will is between reason and bodily appetites and may be moved by either; by reason in the continent man, and by appetites in the incontinent . . . but both motions properly belong to the will as their root" (*Summa Theologiae*, II-II, q. 155, a. 3, ad 2). "All appetites in man—hence not just the irascible and the concupiscible, but certainly the will also—participate in man's rationality" (Ibid., I-II, q. 56, a. 6, ad 2). [My translations]

25 See Mortimer J. Adler, *The Idea of Freedom*, 2 vols. And those uneasy these days about B. F. Skinner's scientific arguments against the reality of free choice in man will find a thoughtful presentation about the dangers of unduly extending the validity of operationalism into the areas of human consciousness and desires in Ricoeur, *Freud and Philosophy*, pp. 352-75.

26 Even though Henri Bergson refuses to ground the act of free choice in rational reflection—as we do here—we can still draw support from his idea on the forward surge of the free act as so purely dynamic as to preclude any authentic account of it except by virtual identification with the agent himself at the very moment of action. For one *is* conscious of making the act of choice, and one can distinguish such an act from all his other acts which are not "choosing." This rules out the external observer, analysts, et al., who watch an act of choice from the outside (itself a questionable claim) and then proceed to sketch out the deterministic antecedents leading to the act. For Bergson on freedom, see *Time and Free Will*, pp. 140-240; also, E. P. Cronan, S.S., "Bergson and Free Will," *The New Scholasticism* 11:1-57, January 1937; S. Cantin, "Henri Bergson et le Probleme de la Liberté," *Laval Theologique et Philosophique* 1:71-102, 1945.

27 Johnstone, *Problem of Self*, p. 68. I have stated this book's thesis in note 1, Chapter II above. The following is also a notion of self very nearly identical to the position I take here, even though the quote is cast in a Bradleyan metaphysics that ultimately precludes my position.

"Human experience is found to imply a unitary and relatively enduring subject, a being not reducible to experiences, but manifesting itself in experiences, a being in which, in the manifestations by which we know it, spirit and body are intermingled and 'compose a certain unity,' yet a being of which the essence is spiritual in the sense that while we can conceive its existence as possible without the body, we can attach no meaning at all to its existence without spirit; a being which, though subject to manifold influences from without, is nevertheless endowed with a creative power which suffices to constitute it a free and responsible agent, master in a real sense of its own destiny; a being, again, which is intrinsically related through its moral consciousness and moral will to an objective order, whereby there is imparted to the life of man on earth a no less cosmic significance; and finally a being that is in some measure, indeed, what it is, but knowing not at all how it is what it is" (C. A. Campbell, *On Selfhood and Godhood*, p. 207). For the individual's meaningful life in a philosophy of totality, see the excellent chapter, "My Station and Its Duties," in Francis H. Bradley, *Ethical Studies*, pp. 98-147.

CHAPTER III

1 An exhaustive study of Love and Strife in Empedocles is found in Denis O'Brien's book, *Empedocles' Cosmic Cycle*.
2 *Symposium*, 190, in Plato, *The Dialogues*, vol. 1, p. 316.
3 Ibid.
4 Ibid.
5 *Nicomachean Ethics*, Book IX, ch. 4, 1166a30, in Aristotle, *Basic Works*, p. 1082. I call the shift from Greek *eros* to Christian *agape* a radical one, because self-interest was so naturally connected to virtue in the Greek mind that not even Socrates questioned this point. What Socrates did probe was where exactly one's genuine self-interest lay. "Greeks normally regarded the good man as a wise man and the criminal as a fool. They seem to have meant by this that virtue is a sort of self-interest. But virtue at times seemed unprofitable, and when it did few Greeks had doctrinaire scruples about calling a villain wise or a good man a fool" (O'Brien, *Socratic Paradoxes*, p. 54). It would be good to compare this sort of selfishness with *The Virtue of Selfishness*, by Ayn Rand.
6 So St. Paul writes to the Philippians: "Have this mind in you which was also in Christ Jesus, who though he was by nature God, did not consider being equal to God a thing to be clung to, but emptied himself, taking the nature of a slave and being made like unto men. And appearing in the form of man, he humbled himself, becoming obedient to death, even to death on a cross" (Philippians 2:5-8).
7 St. Augustine's words on *amor rectus* and *amor curvatus* were these: "Recta itaque voluntas est bonus amor, et voluntas perversa malus amor. . . . Proinde mala sunt ista si malus est amor; bona, si bonus" (*De Civitate Dei*, in *Patrologia Latina*, vol. 41, col. 410). For St. Augustine's teaching on charity, see Eugène Portalié, S.J., *A Guide to the Thought of Saint Augustine*, pp. 270-88; or Etienne Gilson, *The Christian Philosophy of Saint Augustine*, pp. 143-64. Straight love (*amor rectus*) here really means charity. According to Christian doctrine, no one can be saved without charity. Hence it is only a step from here to the controversial question of whether saving grace is totally and unilaterally from God, or whether human effort enters into it. Some sample texts may illustrate why later appeals to St. Augustine, who was ambiguous on this point, merely heightened instead of resolving the controversy.

"But when the soul is cleansed from the world's most sordid affections, with its pair of wings now extended and free from every hindrance, she flies on the two precepts of love of God and love of neighbor. Whereto but to God since she rises in flight by love?" (*Patr. Lat.*, vol. 37, col. 1618 or *Corpus Christianorum: Series Latina*, vol. 40, p. 1801. *Ennarationes in Psalmos*, CXXI, 1).

"Then are sins said to be overcome when they are vanquished by the love of God, which love only God himself gives, and in no other way than through the Mediator between God and man, the man Jesus Christ, who was made a sharer of our mortality so that he may make us sharers of his divinity" (*Patr. Lat.*, vol. 41, col. 730; *Corpus Christ.*, vol. 48, p. 782. *De Civitate Dei*, Book XXI, ch. 16).

"Love of the world by which a man becomes a lover of this world is not from God; I mean, a love that enjoys any creature whatever without the love of its Creator is not from God. Now God's love by which we reach God is not except from God the Father through Jesus Christ with the Holy Spirit" (*Patr. Lat.*, vol. 44, col. 756. *Contra Julianum*, Book IV, ch. 3).

"The word *love* refers either to love of the creature or of the Creator; either to cupidity or to charity, not as though no creature ought to be loved, since if that love is referred to the Creator then it is no longer cupidity but charity. But it is indeed cupidity when a creature is loved for itself" (*Patr. Lat.*, vol. 42, col. 967-78; *Corpus Christ.*, vol. 50, p. 304. *De Trinitate*, Book IX, chs. 7 and 8).

"I call charity that movement of the soul towards enjoying God for his own sake, and one's self and one's neighbor for God's sake. I call cupidity that movement of the soul towards enjoying one's self and one's neighbor and whatever corporeal thing, without reference to God" (*Patr. Lat.*, vol. 34, col. 72; *Corpus Christ.*, vol. 32, p. 87. *De Doctrina Christiana*, III, x, 16).

"God must be loved such that, if it is possible, we should forget ourselves" (*Patr. Lat.*, vol. 38, col. 779. *Sermo*, cxlii).

8 Gerard M. Hopkins, *Poems*, p. 188. Another of Hopkins' poems expresses this theocentric medieval view thus:

> Thee God I come from, to thee go,
> All day long I like fountain flow
> From thy hand out, swayed about
> Mote-like in thy mighty glow (Ibid., p. 167).

And the medieval concept of evildoing may not be so antiquated after all, since we find the contemporary philosopher, Gabriel Marcel, saying: "You will ask what definition of sin can be suggested. What we can say, I think, is that all authentic sin is sin against the light; in other words, against the universal. At root, it is the act of shutting oneself in on oneself, or of taking one's own self as the centre. On this point all great religions seem to be in agreement" (*The Mystery of Being*, vol. 2, p. 203).

9 Anders Nygren, *Agape and Eros*, p. 210.

10 Ibid., p. 682. On Luther's *sola fides* teaching, see "Treatise on Good Works," in Martin Luther, *Works*, vol. 44, pp. 21-114; especially pp. 23-39, where Luther takes up the text of St. Paul's Epistle to the Romans: *"justus ex fide sua vivit."*

11 Nygren, *Agape and Eros*, p. 688. On Luther's view of monastic vows, including his own, as "not worth a fig," see Luther, *Works*, vol. 44, pp. 251-400.

12 Nygren, *Agape and Eros*, p. 703. For Luther's sustained argumentation that man is justified by faith alone, see "The Disputation Concerning Justification," in Luther, *Works*, vol. 34, pp. 151-96.

13 Nygren, *Agape and Eros*, pp. 719-20.

14 Reactions to Nygren's book can be found in: T. S. Gregory, Review of *Agape and Eros, Month* 11:221-34, April 1954, which confronts Nygren's Lutheran thesis; T. Barrose, "The Unity of the Two Charities in Greek Patristic Exegesis," *Theological Studies* 15:355-88, September 1954, which discusses Nygren's claim that the Patristic period witnessed a corruption of

agape with neo-Platonic elements; A. H. Armstrong, "Platonic Eros and Christian Agape," *Downside Review* 79:105-21, September 1961, which argues against dividing *eros* from *agape*. In addition, there are two works which stress the authentic role of human love in its metaphysical relation to God: Robert O. Johann, S.J., *The Meaning of Love*, and Maurice Nédoncelle, *Love and the Person*.

15 Nygren, *Agape and Eros*, p. 684.

16 Ibid., p. 625.

17 Martin D'Arcy, S.J., *The Mind and Heart of Love*, p. 80.

18 Ibid., p. 81.

19 Ibid., p. 354.

20 Pierre Rousselot, *Pour L'Histoire du Problème de L'Amour Au Moyen Age*.

21 Etienne Gilson, *The Spirit of Mediaeval Philosophy*, p. 286.

22 Ibid. Gilson supports his position from the following texts from Aquinas: *In II Sent.*, d. 1, q. 2, ad 2; *Contra Gentiles*, III, cc. 24, 25.

23 Benjamin S. Llamzon, "The Specification of Esse," *The Modern Schoolman* 41:123-43, January 1964; Llamzon, "Supposital and Accidental Esse," *The New Scholasticism* 39:170-88, April 1965; Báñez, *Primacy of Existence in Aquinas*.

24 D'Arcy, *Mind and Heart of Love*, p. 331.

25 Ibid., p. 341.

26 Ibid., p. 344.

27 Ibid., p. 370. Here are some other key texts from D'Arcy.

"In brute creation the life of the individual is not of such importance as to create a real problem. The individual is sacrificed. . . . If reason, the differentiating activity of man, is of its very essence self-regarding, it is very difficult to see how the other love can enter into a person's life. Its counterpart in the animal world could be so insouciant of the self's claim as to make it a mere means to some other object and even sacrifice its life. A person cannot allow this to happen; he must never be a means" (Ibid., p. 358).

"But to judge by the lessons of history, *anima* is sure to prove refractory and to go roaming. The romantic movement, the phases of mysticism and irrationalism, bear witness to this. The only answer, the only true harmony, must be sought in religion—in the communion of *anima* with its divine lover. But even this will fail unless, as in the Christian religion, the divine lover befriends *animus* as well, and gives power to the unavailing soul to be led to the altar of God" (Ibid.).

28 Ibid., p. 343.

"The infinite perfection of the divine Persons demands therefore complete disinterestedness in their mutual relations . . . but the disinterested love which comes from his [man's] being an existing self, while it allows for this self-regarding love, gathers it up in its movement towards that self-subsistent Being of infinite love, from whom its existence has come and to whom it belongs" (Ibid.).

"There is the love which is self-interested and the love which is disinterested. The one is introvert; all is grist to the mill of the essence . . . its business is to adorn nature, however Spartan, to preserve and increase its worth. The other is extrovert; it is not directly concerned with essence . . . it moves away from the limited, unstable life it has towards the existent ground of all being: it hangs on the word of another" (Ibid., p. 344).

29 Ibid., p. 370.

30 Ibid., p. 373.

31 Nygren, *Agape and Eros*, p. vi. A good book to round off this whole discussion on *eros* and *agape*, and which brings the topic down to the nitty-gritty details of everyday problems, joys, pains, and many another human vulnerability linked to loving is C. S. Lewis, *The Four Loves*. What one can perhaps conclude from this whole debate is the realization that reality is neither completely rational (see note 17, Chapter I above) nor so irrational as to be accessible only to "faith." Why can't we take reason as *dialectical*, forever attempting to get at the *coincidence of opposites* glimpsed by it in experiences? One way of interpreting life, shown by dialectical reason itself, is through religious faith. This is a point well made in Howard A. Slaatte, *The Pertinence of the Paradox*.

32 Søren Kierkegaard, *Philosophical Fragments*, p. 33.

33 Søren Kierkegaard, *Concluding Unscientific Postscript*, p. 182. See H. E. Allison's excellent article, "Faith and Falsifiability," *The Review of Metaphysics* 22:508-22, March 1969, which sets up a Kierkegaardian view of reality as a workable dialectical counterpart to the dead-end view of reality that results from the language analysts' demand that statements about the transcendent be "verifiable."

34 Søren Kierkegaard, *Fear and Trembling*, p. 53. See Cole, *Problematic Self*, pp. 11-32, for a good presentation of the self in Kierkegaard existentially mediating itself through imagination toward infinity of Spirit. Cole works out an excellent parallel between the self in Kierkegaard—in its dreaming state of immediacy, in its state of dread ("a sympathetic antipathy and antipathetic sympathy"), and in *repetition*—and the self in Freud considered somatically, then the self in its various pathologies, and finally the self in therapy.

35 Søren Kierkegaard, *The Sickness unto Death*, p. 146.

36 Ibid., pp. 147, 182.

37 Ibid., pp. 244-45.

38 Ibid., p. 211. See also Cole, *Problematic Self*, pp. 11-32, 75-101, 149-74.

39 Kierkegaard, *Sickness unto Death*, p. 234.

40 Søren Kierkegaard, *Works of Love*, p. 116. See also Louis Dupré, "The Constitution of the Self in Kierkegaard's Philosophy," *International Philosophical Quarterly* 3:506-26, December 1963.

41 Bonhoeffer, *Letters from Prison*, pp. 197-98.

42 Ibid., p. 188.

43 Ibid., p. 202.

44 Dietrich Bonhoeffer, *Ethics*, p. 278.

45 Bonhoeffer, *Letters from Prison*, p. 202.

46 Ibid., p. 183.

47 Dietrich Bonhoeffer writes on this point of Christ unifying what was once whole but now fallen into the is/ought (indicative/imperative) division in *Creation and Fall: Temptation*.

48 Bonhoeffer, *Letters from Prison*, p. 60.
49 Ibid., p. 207.

CHAPTER IV

1 Jones, *Life and Work*, vol. 2, p. 291, writes: "Since kissing, v. g., conduces towards more intense excitation, Freud concluded that they must imply a state of tension. Now tension, he always maintained, means 'unpleasure,' since it impels towards discharge and relief. On the other hand, there is no doubt that the acts themselves are pleasurable, and no one wants to bring pleasure to an end. How resolve this antinomy? It was twenty years before Freud was able to find a solution." The solution to which Jones refers is Freud's pivotal work of his late years, *Beyond the Pleasure Principle*, whose main idea is the intertwining of *eros* and *thanatos*. On this problem of equating tension with unpleasure, and discharge of tension along with its consequent equilibrium with pleasure, see Ricoeur, *Freud and Philosophy*, pp. 71-82, 111-14, and especially pp. 261-338. Also see Jones; *Life and Work*, vol. 3, pp. 268-70. One may also note here a parallel to John Dewey's thought that looked upon reality as data for intelligence, not as objects with finished forms (much less eternal forms as the ancients held), to be used instrumentally toward satisfaction. See, for instance, *Experience and Nature*, pp. 85 ff., 98 ff.
2 Sigmund Freud, *Beyond the Pleasure Principle*, in *Standard Edition*, vol. 18, p. 42.
3 See notes 1 and 2, Chapter III above.
4 Freud, *Standard Edition*, vol. 18, p. 57.
5 Ibid., p. 58.
6 Ibid., p. 38.
7 Close readings of Freud have raised the question whether or not the instincts are reducibly one or many in his conception of man. See, for instance, *Standard Edition*, vol. 18, pp. 38, 52, 53, 60-61. Or again Freud writes thus after he has maintained the plurality of instincts: "Over and over again we find, when we are able to trace instinctual impulses back, that they reveal themselves as derivatives of Eros. If it were not for the considerations put forth in *Beyond the Pleasure Principle*, and ultimately for the sadistic constituents which have attached themselves to Eros, we should have difficulty in holding to our fundamental dualistic point of view. But since we cannot escape that view, we are driven to conclude that the death instincts are by their nature mute and that the clamor of life proceeds for the most part from Eros" (Ibid., vol. 19, p. 46). See also *Instincts and Their Vicissitudes*, in Ibid., vol. 14, pp. 113-16; and vol. 21, pp. 59-63; also David Bakan, *The Duality of Human Existence*, pp. 154-96. Ernest Jones takes Freud's thought on this matter as definitely dualistic, even though Federn, not Freud, was the first to use the word *thanatos* for the death instinct. See Jones, *Life and Work*, vol. 3, pp. 267, 273, 274-80. Jones writes: "In reply to a question whether he regarded the pleasure principle and the reality principle as distinct, or, as I supposed, the latter only as an extension of the former, Freud wrote me: 'The reality principle

is only continuing the work of the pleasure principle in a more effectual way, gratification being the aim of both, and their opposition only a secondary fact. Yet, I am sure this paper of mine will produce much hesitation and wants a better thorough-going exposition" (Ibid., vol. 2, p. 453). This may be one instance of Freud's dislike for precise definitions, a characteristic of his which he called *schlamperei* ("sloppiness") (Ibid., vol. 1, p. 34).

8 Freud, *Standard Edition*, vol. 18, p. 38.

9 Jones, *Life and Work*, vol. 2, p. 289; Freud, *Totem and Taboo*, in *Standard Edition*, vol. 13, p. 90. In his last work, *Moses and Monotheism* (*Standard Edition*, vol. 18, pp. 72-80), Freud still talks of this phase, up to the age of five years old, as the transitional stage toward universal traumas.

10 Ibid., and see note 21, Chapter II above.

11 Marcuse, *Eros and Civilization*, "Political Preface," p. xv. Marcuse's attack is ultimately against institutions which are, after all, established and protected by law, so one would have expected lawyers to turn their attention on him. Instead there is almost total silence from barristers on Marcuse. William Stanmeyer, writing from a conservative viewpoint, explores this phenomenon in an extensive article, "The Jurisprudence of Radical Change: Herbert Marcuse's 'Great Refusal' Vs. Political Due Process," *St. John's Law Review* 45:1-38, October 1970.

12 In *Civilization and Its Discontents* (*Standard Edition*, vol. 18, p. 113), Freud discusses private property, human aggression, and communism, which he calls an "untenable illusion." Then he writes: "Aggressiveness was not created by property. It reigned almost without limit in primitive times, when property was still scanty, and it already shows itself in the nursery almost before property has given up its primal, anal form; it forms the basis of every relation of affection and love among people. If we do away with personal rights over material wealth, there still remains prerogative in the field of sexual relationships. . . . If we were to remove this factor, too, by allowing complete freedom of sexual life and thus abolishing the family, the germ-cell of civilization, we cannot, it is true, easily foresee what new paths the development of civilization could take; but one thing we could expect, and that is that this indestructible feature of human nature will follow it there." Freud's words seem especially timely these days when marriage as an institution is up for so much reevaluation, as we shall see in Chapter VI.

13 See Friedrich Nietzsche, *Thus Spake Zarathustra*, "The Drunken Song," in *Portable Nietzsche*, pp. 429-35.

14 Philip Rieff, *The Triumph of the Therapeutic*, p. 21. For an evaluation of Rieff's book, see William F. Lynch, "Psychological Man," *America* 117:635-37, November 25, 1967. Lynch writes: "It has, on the contrary, been the experience of Western culture and history that there is no part of man, no matter how inward, that is locked off from aggression and hate, and that, in fact, the deeper you go into his interior the more you are apt to find these demons at their worst. The external forms of democracy regularly collapse as often as they are built on people who are not interiorly free. The external forms of peace will collapse if they are not built on people who have inward peace or at least wish peace or know they do not

have inward peace. The harmless interior kingdom of the self seems the latest delusion."

15 Rieff, *Triumph of the Therapeutic*, p. 59.

16 Ibid., p. 252. While it is true that God and religion were constantly under attack in all of Freud's writings, there were occasional evidences of a theoretical and practical nature that show Freud short of dogmatic on the whole matter. The most compelling evidence, as Jones notes, is the careful distinction he made between "illusion" and "delusion," when he used the former word as the title of his attack on religion: *Die Zukunft einer Illusion* (The Future of an Illusion). Here he explicitly says that an illusion may or may not be true, while a delusion is altogether false. One discerns the same cold attitude of rejection in at least three other places of many where Freud uses the word "illusion": (1) man, as basically good and noble, is called a *wöhltuende illusion* ("benevolent illusion") (*Gesammelte Werke*, vol. 13, p. 44 and *Standard Edition*, vol. 18, p. 42); (2) where he talks of communism, as in note 12, Chapter IV above, as untenable, *haltlöse illusion* ("untenable illusion") (*Gesammelte Werke*, vol. 14, p. 473); (3) in *Moses and Monotheism* (*Standard Edition*, vol. 23, p. 129), where illusion is coupled with wish: *wunschillusion* ("wishful illusion") (*Gesammelte Werke*, vol. 16, p. 238). We do have accounts, though, of Freud occasionally mystifying his friends on the question of God. We know that he loved Rome, going there seven times, and dreaming of settling there, while protesting all the while "the great lie of salvation." Once he told Binswanger, "*Ja, Geist ist alles*" ("Yes, spirit is everything"), and then quickly explained the statement away, but one should notice that the statement did "slip through" from the very man who convinced the world that nothing of this import slips through groundlessly. See Ludwig Binswanger, *Sigmund Freud: Reminiscences of a Friendship*, pp. 80-81; also Jones, *Life and Work*, vol. 3, p. 381. However, Freud's final word on this matter is categorical: "As an unbelieving fatalist I can only let my arms sink before the terrors of death" (Ibid., p. 140). And just before his death, he wrote Marie Bonaparte, ". . . and I hope you will soon console yourself over my death and let me go on living in your friendly recollections—the only kind of limited immortality I recognize" (Ibid., p. 465).

17 This is the theme of Herbert Marcuse's book, *One Dimensional Man*.

18 Brown, *Life Against Death*, p. 108.

19 Christiaan Neethling Barnard and C. B. Pepper, *Christiaan Barnard: One Life*, p. 89. See also Nietzsche, *Thus Spake Zarathustra*, "On Free Death," in *Portable Nietzsche*, pp. 183-86: "Die at the proper time. . . . All ascribe importance to their dying; but death has not yet become an occasion to celebrate. I show you a death which is a fulfillment; he who is fulfilled dies his death. . . . Each man must take leave of his honors at the right time and practice the difficult art of leaving in time. . . . I recommend to you my death, free death, which comes because I wish it to come."

20 Here are starkly contrasting texts from Berdyaev and Freud.

Nicolas Berdyaev: "Meaning is never revealed in an endless time; it is to be found in eternity. But there is an abyss between life in time and life in eternity, and it can only be bridged by death and the horror of final severance. When this world is apprehended as self-sufficient, completed and closed in, everything in it appears meaningless because everything is transitory and corruptible—i.e., death and mortality in this world is just what makes it meaningless. This is one-half of the truth seen from a narrow and limited point of view. Heidegger is right in saying that herd-mentality (*das man*) is insensitive to the anguish of death. It feels merely a low fear of death as that which makes life meaningless. But there is also another half of the truth concealed from the ordinary point of view. Death not merely makes life senseless and corruptible; it is also a sign, coming from the depths, of there being a higher meaning in life. Not base fear but horror and anguish which death inspires in us prove that we belong not only to the surface but to the depths as well. While we are in time, eternity both attracts and horrifies us" (*The Destiny of Man*, p. 250). See also Bakan, *Duality of Human Existence*, pp. 197-236, on the Judaeo-Christian tradition of coming to terms with death.

Now Freud: "Life is impoverished, it loses its interest, when the highest stake in the game of living, life itself, may not be risked" (*Collected Papers*, vol. 4, p. 306). "It becomes as flat, as superficial as those American flirtations in which it is understood from the first that nothing is to happen, contrasted to a Continental love affair in which both partners must constantly bear in mind the serious consequences" (Ibid.).

21 Alfred Lord Tennyson, *Tithonus*, lines 1-10, in *Complete Poetical Works.*

22 Brown, *Life Against Death*, p. 308. Brown continues his thought in another book, *Love's Body*, specifically the ending chapters, "Resurrection," "Fulfillment," etc., pp. 191-255.

23 Gabriel Marcel, *Philosophy of Existence*, p. 5. At this point, our dialectical contrast should perhaps swing over from the Freudians to Pierre Teilhard de Chardin. I have three reasons for not doing so. (1) It will lengthen this book beyond its limit. (2) It will move me into a scientific area distinct from the humanistic-philosophical discourse of this book. (3) One is stopped cold in philosophizing by statements like this: "If this book is to be properly understood, it must be read not as a work on metaphysics, still less as a sort of theological essay, but purely and simply as a scientific treatise. Of set purpose, I have at all times carefully avoided venturing into that field of the essence of being" (*The Phenomenon of Man*, p. 29; also p. 58, and the note on p. 169). If one objects that these were merely strategic remarks of a living and faithful Jesuit, one must yet concede that the problem is one of *fidelity*, my precise topic here. Can the writer of a deep spiritual book, *The Divine Milieu*, say one thing consistently and mean something else all the time? At any rate, the interested reader can read a book on man built along Teilhard's thoughts in J. F. Donceel, S.J., *Philosophical Anthropology*, specifically especially pp. 71-85, and pp. 54-55 for Donceel's opinion that Teilhard changed his position on the scope of the term "science."

24 Marcel, *Philosophy of Existence*, p. 5. See also Kenneth Gallagher, *The Philosophy of Gabriel Marcel*, p. 52, and Marcel, *Presence and Immortality*, pp. 233-35.

25 Marcel, *Philosophy of Existence*, p. 16.

26 Gabriel Marcel, *Creative Fidelity*, pp. 12, 89, 91.

27 Ibid., p. 167.

28 Ibid., pp. 40-43.

29 Gallagher, *Philosophy of Marcel*, p. 78.

30 Marcel, *Mystery of Being*, vol. 2, p. 169.

31 Gabriel Marcel, *Homo Viator*, pp. 152-53; also Marcel, *Creative Fidelity*, p. 149. We should keep Marcel's distinctions in mind. We are talking of "communion and presence" here, not the objective presence of things nor even the "communication of words transmitted and heard" without any real union among the communicants. What Marcel calls *communion* takes place in "grace and light" (*Presence and Immortality*, pp. 236-44).

    "The presence I am thinking of is supra-hypothetical; it gives rise to an invincible assurance which is connected with oblative love. It expresses itself by some such affirmations as: 'I am assured that you are present to me, and this assurance is linked with the fact that you do not stop helping me, that you help me perhaps more directly than you could on earth. We are together in the light. More exactly, in moments when I am detached from myself, when I cease to eclipse myself, I gain access to a light which is your light . . . in which you yourself blossom, that which you help to reflect or radiate upon me . . .'" (Ibid., p. 242).

32 Gallagher, *Philosophy of Marcel*, p. 112.

33 Ibid., p. 62. Some essays on this point in Marcel are: Mary Schaldenbrand, "Self-Becoming and the Other," *Thought* 41:413-37, Autumn 1966; Schaldenbrand, "Gabriel Marcel: Philosopher of Intersubjectivity," in *Twentieth-Century Thinkers*, pp. 107-30; Schaldenbrand, "Freedom and the I," *International Philosophical Quarterly* 3:571-99, December 1963; Schaldenbrand, "Time, the Self and Hope," in *The Future as the Presence of Shared Hope*, pp. 112-29; Donald J. Siewert, "The Body in Marcel's Metaphysics," *Thought* 46:389-405, Autumn 1971; Clyde Pax, "Philosophical Reflection: Gabriel Marcel," *The New Scholasticism* 38:159-77, April 1964. See also Sadler, *Existence and Love*, pp. 95-114.

34 C. S. Lewis, *A Grief Observed*, p. 59.

35 Cf. Robert G. Hazo, *The Idea of Love*. This book is the most comprehensive compilation to date of the various theories of love in western thought. The themes on love of forty-four thinkers across the ages are summarized and documented here with scarcely any editorial intervention, so to speak, for such a massive task.

36 Jules Toner, S.J., *The Experience of Love*.

37 Ibid., p. 12.

38 Ibid., p. 134.

39 Ibid., p. 136.

40 Ibid., p. 148.

41 Ibid., p. 151.

42 Ibid., p. 183.

43 Marcel, *Creative Fidelity*, p. 114.

44 Nédoncelle, *Love and the Person*, pp. 19-20.

CHAPTER V

1 Emmanuel Levinas, *Totality and Infinity*, passim.

2 Ibid., pp. 222-25, and passim. Ludwig Wittgenstein uses the face to illustrate the mingling of commonness and particularity, as in his statement, "This face has a quite particular expression." (See the note on p. 66 of his *Philosophical Investigations*.) There is indeed such a thing as a "family face," with perhaps ten outstanding features. Yet not all those ten features need be present before a relative with several of them can be said to have "the family face."

3 Maurice Merleau-Ponty, *Phenomenology of Perception*, pp. 183-84. See pp. 360-61 for thoughts on the gaze of the stranger with a sense of intentionality other than the one I am using here. To grasp Merleau-Ponty's use of the word "transcendence" in these pages, one needs to enter into his thought on that "living connection" to (p. 205), and "primal acquisition" of (p. 216), that primordial layer in which things and ideas come into being, something he keeps pointing to in his book.

4 Levinas, *Totality and Infinity*, pp. 91-92.

5 Rollo May, *Love and Will*, p. 241. For a lucid analysis of "meaninglessness" see Edward Erwin, *The Concept of Meaninglessness*. Erwin presents clear refutations of philosophies that restrict "meaning" to the empirical, to the operational, etc. He then argues for his own concept of "a priori false," i.e., "if the negation of a true statement is false, then it follows that all putatively meaningless statements (except for those which are true) are false. Hence there are no meaningless statements in the sense in which 'meaninglessness' means neither true nor false. For instance, the negation of 'virtue is square' is both meaningless and false because it is 'not only true but also unintelligible, since we cannot understand what it would be like for it to be true'" (Ibid., pp. 136, 138).

6 May, *Love and Will*, p. 241.

7 On virtues interconnected among themselves through prudence, see Aquinas, *Summa Theologiae*, I-II, q. 65, a. 1; II-II, q. 47, a. 5; see also note 25, Chapter V below. In Plato, this reduction is effected through the essential unity of genuine human knowledge (*episteme*), even though the question of the One coming or not coming into relationship with the Other remained aporetic; see the dialogue *Parmenides*. In Aristotle, the concept of friendship (*Nicomachean Ethics*, Books VIII and IX) is presented as exclusively enjoyed only by virtuous men among themselves. There is a reductive unity here in that a friend first of all loves the life of reason in himself, and then loves this same life of reason in the other, who is thus literally his *alter ego*, another I. Accordingly, one life of reason dwells in friends and is loved by them reflectively among themselves—the best mortal analogate Aristotle could find for God as self-confined reflective Thinking, "a thinking of thinking upon thinking" (*Metaphysics*, Book XII, ch. 9). Among medievals, we find Aquinas again explicitly raising the question whether virtue is one and concluding at least to the orderly enchainment of virtue, with charity

as the archetectonic crowning point (*Summa Theologiae*, I-II, q. 65, articles 2, 3, 4, 5). The basic unity of human goodness when it is achieved seems to be a recurrent insight. A very simple and literal illustration of this point is had, for instance, in Milton Mayeroff's little book, *On Caring*. He shows how a host of other virtues are present when one truly "cares." For a unique view of this problem as it appears in Plato's *Protagoras*, see Gregory Vlastos, "The Unity of the Virtues in the *Protagoras*," *The Review of Metaphysics* 25:415-58, March 1972.

8 Gottfried W. Leibniz, *New Essays Concerning the Human Understanding*, Appendix X, pp. 714-15.

9 Maurice Natanson, *The Journeying Self*, p. 63. See also Erving Goffman, *Behavior in Public Places*; Nicolai Berdiaev, *Solitude and Society*, pp. 125 ff. The view of the self as *ultima solitudo* is in the medieval thinker Duns Scotus (*Oxon.*, 3, D. 1, n. 17). In *Religion in the Making*, Alfred N. Whitehead makes the intriguing remark that "religion is what a man does with his own solitariness." He then goes on to give an interesting resolution between the essential solitariness of a genuine religious spirit and social rituals. "The emergence of rational religion was strictly conditioned by the general progress of the races in which it arose. It has to wait for the development of human consciousness of the relevant ideas and of the relevant ethical intuitions. It required that such ideas should not merely be casually entertained by isolated individuals, but that they should be stabilized in recognizable forms of expression, so as to be recalled and communicated. *You can only speak of mercy among a people who, in some respects, are already merciful*" (Ibid., p. 16). [Italics added] Whitehead continues, ". . . expression is the one fundamental sacrament. . . . But the expressive sign is more than interpretable. It is creative. It elicits the intuition which interprets it. It cannot elicit what is not there. A note on a tuning fork can elicit a response from a piano. But the piano already has in it the string tuned to the same note. In the same way, the expressive sign elicits the existent intuition which would not otherwise emerge into individual distinctiveness. Again, in the theological language, the sign works *ex opere operato*, but only within the limitation that the recipient be patient of the creative action" (Ibid., pp. 132-33). For a *tour de force* on being related in order to be solitary, see P. Munz, *Relationship and Solitude*.

10 Camus, *Myth of Sisyphus*, p. 132.

11 Gabriel Marcel, *Being and Having*, pp. 211-12.

12 Miguel de Cervantes, *Don Quixote*, p. 443.

13 Freud, *Standard Edition*, vol. 11, p. 149. See also Philip Rieff, *Freud: The Mind of the Moralist*, p. 316.

14 Rieff, *Freud: Mind of the Moralist*, p. 316.

15 Ibid., p. 121.

16 Freud, *Standard Edition*, vol. 18, p. 123; and vol. 23, pp. 132-37. Also Rieff, *Triumph of the Therapeutic*, pp. 143, 151, 193 ff., and Marcuse, *Eros and Civilization*, pp. 16 ff., 89, 212. To the questions: Is civilization really constituted by the polarity of freedom and repression, productivity and destruction, domination and progress? Are pleasure and reality princi-

ples so irreconcilable as to necessitate the repressive transformation of man's instinctual structure? Is a nonrepressive civilization with fundamentally different relations between men and nature, between men themselves, possible? Marcuse replies: "Freud's theoretical conception itself seems to refute his consistent denial of the historical possibility of a nonrepressive civilization . . . the very achievement of a repressive civilization seems to create the preconditions for the gradual abolition of repression" (*Eros and Civilization*, p. 5). See also his essay "Repressive Tolerance" in *A Critique of Pure Tolerance*, pp. 81-123.

17 See Paul Roazen, "A Curious Triangle: Freud, Lou Andreas-Salomé and Victor Tausk," *Encounter* 33:83-89, October 1969. On this matter Ernest Jones writes: "Freud had a black and white judgement of people, good and bad, or perhaps more accurately into liked and disliked, with very little in between. And the same person could move from one category into the other from time to time. He was a poor *Menschenkenner*—a poor judge of men. His emotions could bias his intellect" (*Life and Work*, vol. 2, p. 412). One who reads Jones' volumes and sees there how Freud's friends vied for his esteem and professional gifts, v. g., translations of his works, can understand why the often embattled Freud looked like a poor *Menschenkenner*. We have already noted how Freud dismissed the conception that humanity was evolving into a race of moral supermen as a "benevolent illusion" (*Standard Edition*, vol. 18, p. 42). Moreover, Jones comments that the meaning-of-life question for Freud had "strictly speaking, no meaning, being founded on unjustifiable premises; as he had pointed out, it is seldom raised in respect to the animal world. So he turned to the more modest question of what human behaviour reveals as its aim. This seemed to him to be indisputably the search for happiness" (*Life and Work*, vol. 3, p. 340). Jones opines that Freud's childhood poverty and its accompanying humiliations were probably behind this attitude of being a "cheerful pessimist" about human beings who, with rare exceptions, were "riff-raff with little good in them" (Ibid., pp. 334-35). It is disappointing to see Freud so apparently oblivious of the point Immanuel Kant made so forcefully that human happiness is so individual in content that, even if one were ever able to arrive at a universal formula for happiness, it would in no way show the object of human desire to be universalizable, but simply open to "inclination as yawning is by seeing others yawn" (*Critique of Practical Reason*, p. 25).

18 As a quick illustration of this controversy from ancient times to our own, see Plato's "Myth of Gyges" in *The Republic* (Book II, pp. 360 ff.) in contrast to Aristotle's concept of the self in Book IX of *Nicomachean Ethics* as "the most authoritative element in a man"; then Nygren propounding Luther's concept of man (as in our previous chapter) in contrast to D'Arcy and Jared Wicks' recent book on Luther, *Man Yearning for Grace*. We have Hobbes' lupine man, Freud's primal horde constructs. Or Ardrey and Lorenz (even granting the paradox in the latter's example of a beast being automatically pacified by his victim's exposure of the jugular at the critical moment of defeat) refuted by Ashley Montagu and other scientists in *Man and Aggression* and in Desmond Morris' book with the deliciously apt title, *The Human Zoo*.

19 Ernest Becker, "The Evaded Question: Science and Human Nature," *Commonweal* 89:650, February 21, 1969.

20 Ibid., p. 641.

21 Leo N. Tolstoy, "My Religion," in *Novels and Other Works*, vol. 17, p. 88.

22 Albert Camus, *The Plague*, pp. 120 ff.

23 The following is a concise statement of St. Thomas' view of man: "The soul simultaneously communicates intentional existence to its powers of apprehension and appetite, and physical existence to such principles as primary matter, quantity, material qualities, and so forth. To put it another way: our apprehensive and appetitive powers limit the communication of existence to be only intentional, and primary matter limits it to be only physical. But as in the soul itself, existence must be both at once. Thus our act of existing, which is actuating the soul and through the soul all that is not the soul, must transcend the source of actuation, material and immaterial, physical and intentional, substantial and accidental existence. It is all of these at once on the level of human existence, just as God is all existence infinitely. This reduction of all our perfections to the act of existence gives unity and synthesis to [St. Thomas'] philosophy of man" (Maurice R. Holloway, S.J., "Towards the Fullness of Being," in *Proceedings, Jesuit Philosophical Association*, 1962, pp. 19-20). See also St. Thomas' rejection of Plato's view of man: *"haec opinio stare non potest"* etc. in *Quaestio Unica De Anima*, a. 1; and A. C. Pegis, *At the Origins of the Thomistic Notion of Man*; also St. Thomas Aquinas, *Treatise on Man*, translated by James F. Anderson.

24 Surprisingly, Descartes' biographers are usually silent about this episode in his life. The official documents on Francine, Descartes' illegitimate daughter whom he dearly loved and who died at a tender age, are cited by C. Adam, in René Descartes, *Vie et Oeuvres*, vol. 12, pp. 575-77. Francine's mother was a Dutch woman, Helene.

25 In many men the tendency to seek meaning in life is the precise point of insertion for religious faith. Is meaning uncovered, "found," "created" by men's freedom, etc.? One clear contrast to the classical notion of meaning as corresponding to reality is in Leslie Dewart's idea of truth as syntactic, evolutionary, functional, etc., as proposed in his three works: *The Future of Belief; The Foundations of Belief; Religion, Language, and Truth*. On inserting faith into life, Dewart writes: ". . . consciousness is not enclosed by that which it itself is, or by that object which it is conscious of. Consciousness transcends not only itself; it transcends itself precisely as being; it transcends being as such. This is why disclosure of that which transcends being is at the same time also the disclosure of man's deepest reality to himself. In this sense awareness of the reality which transcends being may be said to be that which reveals to man the meaning of his existence. What existence reveals is that the meaning of existence is not to be found within existence itself, but beyond. To conceptualize positively that reality which transcends being, 'presence' seems to me particularly apt" (*Foundations of Belief*, pp. 441-42).

26 See Domingo Báñez, *Scholastica Commentaria in Primam Partem S.T.*, Reprinted Edition, pp. 7-99; or Etienne Gilson, *The Christian Philosophy of*

St. Thomas Aquinas, pp. 3-25, where the scholastic positions on faith and reason are discussed.

27 Here are some key texts:

"As for knowing the particulars which are involved in a concrete action, we may see them either as an end or the means to an end. Now the right ends of human life are fixed; hence there can be a natural inclination in respect of these ends; thus it has been stated above (I-II, q. 51, a. 1; q. 63, articles 1 & 2) that some men, from a natural inclination, have certain virtues whereby they are inclined to right ends, consequently they also have naturally a right judgment about such like ends. But the means to the end, in human concerns, are not fixed, and are as manifold and various as persons and human situations. Since the inclination of nature is ever to something fixed, the knowledge of those means then cannot be in man naturally, even though because of his natural disposition one man may have a greater aptitude than another in discerning them, just as it happens with regard to the conclusions of speculative sciences. Since then prudence is not about ends, but about the means as stated above (a. 6; I-II, q. 57, a. 5), it follows that prudence is not from nature" (*Summa Theologiae*, II-II, q. 47, a. 15, c.). Aquinas then goes on: "Now prudence is in the old, not only because their natural disposition calms down the movement of the sensitive passions, but also because of their knowledge from long experience" (Ibid., ad 2).

"I answer that the virtues are necessarily interconnected so that whoever has one has all, as stated above (I-II, q. 65, a. 1). Now whoever has grace has charity, and so too all the other virtues. Hence since prudence is a virtue as shown above (a. 4), he must of necessity have prudence also" (Ibid., q. 47, a. 1). [My translations]

See also Charles de Koninck, "General Standards and Particular Situations in Relation to Natural Law," in *Proceedings, American Catholic Philosophical Association*, vol. 24, 1950, pp. 28-32.

28 On this point Aquinas is blunt about fostering the good in the other through imprudent communication. In *Summa Theologiae*, II-II, q. 115, a. 1, we find this objection: "Evil is contrary to good and blame contrary to praise. But it is not a sin to blame evil. Neither then is it a sin to praise good, and yet is this not flattery?" Aquinas replies: "*Even to blame evil is sinful, if due circumstances be not observed; and so too is it to praise good.*" [My translations, italics added] My point here revolves on this prudent communication to foster the *admirable* in the other (and thus necessarily also in oneself) as crucial to the wholing process. For is it not admirable in one to foster the admirable in the other? If one opens the floodgates by pressing the relative character of what is *admirable*, I can only reply that Camus, from whom I take the idea, gives quite specific instances and unmistakable descriptions of what this *admirable* is in human interactions—and by implication, what it is not. There is something wrong with this attempt to reduce the *admirable* to the *despicable* through the abstract concept of relativization, an instance again, it seems to me, of Whitehead's "fallacy of misplaced concreteness."

29 Robert J. Lifton, "The Young and the Old," *The Atlantic Monthly* 224:51, September 1969.
30 Ibid., p. 47.

CHAPTER VI

1 "Is not any promise rooted in a state of mind which is entirely of the moment and whose permanence nothing can guarantee?" (Marcel, *Being and Having*, p. 51). The problem, as Marcel sees it, is that to carry through externally the promise I make, v.g., to visit a dying friend daily, does not really fulfill it if my inner disposition has changed to the contrary. "Is it not just as ridiculous as pledging myself to vote for the Conservative candidate if I become a Socialist before polling-day?" (Ibid., p. 43). Yet how can one promise his inward disposition, over which he obviously has no complete control? Marcel uses this human experience of fidelity as his pathway toward attesting to a Being greater than man, namely God, in whose presence human commitments and bonds are grounded.
2 Thornton Wilder, *Three Plays*, "The Skin of Our Teeth," Act II, pp. 200-01.
3 Dennis Doherty, "Consummation and the Indissolubility of Marriage," in *Absolutes in Moral Theology?* pp. 211-31.
4 Ibid., p. 222.
5 Denis de Rougemont, *Passion and Society*, p. 134. There is no history of happy love in European literature, says De Rougemont. "Love and death, fatal love . . . sums up if not the whole of poetry, at least whatever is popular, whatever is universally moving in European literature in its oldest legend and sweetest song. . . . The word 'adultery' sums up one half of human unhappiness" (Ibid., p. 15). One half? Should not one take into consideration what makes news and what is taken for granted? At the beginning of *Anna Karenina*, Leo Tolstoy writes: "All happy families are alike, but an unhappy family is unhappy after its own fashion" (p. 13). De Rougemont's thesis in his book is that Europe was in fact deeply pagan and still non-Christian at heart in the troubadour years of the twelfth century. Yet the Catholic Church had triumphed and rulers had imposed the faith forcibly on Europe. So these pagan sentiments had to go into hiding and resort to symbolic speech—hence the allegories in courtly tales. What were the courtly tales about? Illicit love. But "illicit" in the eyes of whom? The Catholic Church, says De Rougemont (himself a non-Catholic), which by making marriage one and indissoluble had perverted the nature of true love which is *free*? Hence some Protestants held that *Roma* was the inversion of *amor*, and German still has the verb *freien* related to marriage. Similarly, the game of chess originated in India with four kings, but in Europe during the twelfth century the queen was made all powerful, while the king was reduced to one move at a time (*Passion and Society*, pp. 111-12). For a good definition of courtly love, see C. S. Lewis, *The Allegory of Love*, pp. 2-3. A reasonable selection in the vast bibliography of courtly love would be the following: Etienne Gilson, "St. Bernard and Courtly Love," in *The Mystical Theology of Saint Bernard*, Appendix IV, pp. 170-97, in which Gilson probes the dispute over whether Catholic

mysticism, specifically as in St. Bernard, inspired or was inspired by courtly love. He maintains: "St. Bernard may have largely contributed to the decadence of the courtly ideal, but never in him could it have found its inspiration" (Ibid., p. 197). The question is significant, since the mystical poetries of the Spanish mystics, whom Unamuno considers Spain's greatest contribution to western civilization, is full of the theme of forbidden love. Gilson notes that while the trouvère and bon vivant Thibaut de Champagne was sounding forth effusions of an ascetic, his "obesity was the chief obstacle he had to overcome in order to attain perfect love" (Ibid., p. 172). See also Amy R. Kelly, *Eleanor of Aquitaine and the Four Kings*; Curtis H. Walker, *Eleanor of Aquitaine*; Mary M. Shideler, *The Theology of Romantic Love: A Study in the Writings of Charles Williams*; Jeffrey B. Russell, "Courtly Love as Religious Dissent," *Catholic Historical Review* 51:31-44, April 1965; John H. Fisher, "Tristan and Courtly Adultery," *Comparative Literature* 9:150-64, Spring 1967. Also see Herman Hughes, S.J., "This Mediaeval Winter," *America* 120:156-58, February 8, 1969, for a comparison between youthful life-styles today and the courtly love tradition, even though Hughes marries Eleanor of Aquitaine (portrayed in the recent film *The Lion in Winter*) to Philip of France, when in fact her French husband was Louis VII; and Herbert W. Richardson, *Nun, Witch, Playmate*, on the evolution of human sexuality from the purely instinctual to the romantic to the eroticization of society including the "uniquely American phenomenon of petting" similar to courtly love, as well as for a study of witchcraft as the antidote to the Lady and to the Virgin Mary.

6 De Rougemont, *Passion and Society*, p. 17.

7 Søren Kierkegaard, *Either/Or*, vol. 1, pp. 75-81; vol. 2, pp. 5-129. See also Reidar Thomte, *Kierkegaard's Philosophy of Religion*, p. 32; and Walter Lowrie who writes of Kierkegaard: "There is no other author but Dante that has so much to say about love (from the aesthetic, the ethical, and the religious points of view), and no other has so ably defended the monogamous ideal of marriage, which is not only a Christian ideal, but the custom of the Germanic peoples" (*Kierkegaard*, p. 284).

8 Arthur Schopenhauer, *The World as Will and Idea*, vol. 3, p. 374; see also ch. XLIV, "The Metaphysics of the Love of the Sexes" (Ibid., pp. 336-75).

9 See Kenneth Clark, *Civilisation*, p. 190, for a discussion of St. Teresa's divine ecstasy, i.e., Bernini's sculpture; also H. W. Janson and D. J. Janson, *History of Art*, p. 408.

10 In *Sex in America*, edited by H. A. Grunwald, Mary Calderone writes: "In the repeated sexual act within marriage, a man and a woman are saying to each other, 'I chose you once above all others, and I choose you again. I'll choose you tomorrow and the next year and the year after that when you are 40 or 50 or 60, and neither of us is any longer so attractive' " (pp. 145-46). And again: "Outside of marriage, the sex act may mean this for a while, but it cannot continue to mean it indefinitely. . . . Only within the self-sought marriage bond can two people create for themselves the security of peace and solitude and time . . . a lifetime . . . by which they can accomplish that which is pivotal and central to all else—namely, total communion" (Ibid., p. 146). Finally: "Make no mistake, there is no

possibility of having a sexual relationship without irrevocably meshing a portion of your two nonphysical selves. . . . How many times, and how casually, are you willing to invest a portion of your total self, and to be the custodian of a like investment from the other person without the sureness of knowing that these investments are being made for keeps?" (Ibid., p. 147).

11 Anne Martin, "Time To Grow in Love," in *What Modern Catholics Think about Birth Control*, p. 198.

12 John A. T. Robinson, *Christian Morals Today*, p. 45.

13 Peter Bertocci, *Sex, Love, and the Person*, p. 121.

14 Here are some texts expressing this theme in John Dewey, a theme he elaborates in the specific area of ethics in *Theory of the Moral Life*, especially chs. V and VI.

"Every situation or field of consciousness is marked by initiation, direction or intent, and consequences or import. What is unique is not these traits, but the property of awareness or perception. Because of this property, the initial stage is capable of being judged in the light of its probable course and consequence. There is anticipation. Each successive event being a stage in the serial process, is both expectant and commemorative. What is more precisely pertinent to our present theme, the terminal outcome when anticipated (as it is when a moving cause of affairs is perceived) becomes an end-in-view, an aim, purpose, a prediction usable as a plan in shaping the course of events" (*Experience and Nature*, p. 101).

"Health is not in itself an end of any natural process; much less an end-in-itself. It is an enjoyed good when it happens, just as disease is a suffered ill. Similarly, truth of belief and statement is an affair that has the quality of good; but it is not an end just because it is good; it becomes an end only when, because of its goodness, it is actively sought for and reached as a conclusion. On this basis, all ends are ends-in-view; they are no longer ideal as characters of Being, as they were when they were in Greek theory, but are the objects of conscious intent" (Ibid., pp. 111-12).

See also Sidney Hook, "The Desirable and Emotive in Dewey's Ethics," in *John Dewey, Philosopher of Science and Freedom*, pp. 194-216; Herbert W. Schneider and Darnell Rucker, "Dewey's Ethics," in *Guide to the Works of John Dewey*, pp. 99-130; S. Morris Eames, "Dewey's Theory of Valuation," in *Guide to the Works of John Dewey*, pp. 183-99. The University of Illinois is publishing the most critical, complete, and comprehensive series of Dewey's works. Of the five volumes now out, volumes 3 and 4 are Dewey's early ethical writings.

15 Emily Brontë, *Wuthering Heights*, pp. 97-98. See also the admittedly inconsistent, yet humane, compromise on the notion of indissolubility held by the Greek Orthodox Church in an essay by Alexander Schmemann, "The Indissolubility of Marriage: The Theological Tradition of the East," in *The Bond of Marriage*, pp. 97-116.

CHAPTER VII

1 D'Arcy, *Mind and Heart of Love*, p. 354.

2 See also, for instance, the story of Maximilian Kolbe, a Franciscan priest who volunteered to die in place of a family man condemned by prison camp

officials to die as a reprisal for an escaped prisoner in Auschwitz in 1941, in *L'Osservatore Romano*, October 18-19, 1971 (English translation of this paper, October 21, 1971). The issue shows pictures of the beatification rites for Kolbe at St. Peter's in Rome and includes a picture of Francis Gajowniczek, the man Kolbe saved, weeping on the pope's shoulder at one point in the ceremonies. An account in English of Kolbe's life can be found in *The Death Camp Proved Him Real*, by Prow Publishers, Kenosha, Wisconsin, 1971, by anyone willing to overlook a rather too devotional presentation.

3 Camus, *Myth of Sisyphus*, p. 40. See also Bernard Murchland, "Between Solitude and Solidarity," *Commonweal* 93:91-95, October 23, 1970.

4 There is a good deal of beautiful material for reflection, on this point of accepting and developing one's own distinctive self, in Martin Buber's religious stories in *Tales of the Hasidim*.

5 Bonhoeffer, *Ethics*, pp. 258, 268.

6 See note 8, Chapter I above.

7 Marcel, *Creative Fidelity*, p. 53.

8 This was the whole point in Chapter I above. On the eschatological versus the incarnational viewpoints, see John Courtney Murray, S.J., "Is It Basket Weaving," in *We Hold These Truths*, pp. 175-96. He uses there the example of how some early monks of the eastern desert spent their lives constantly weaving baskets by day and unweaving them each night simply to keep busy—idleness being the devil's workshop!—all the time convinced that what one did in time or this earthly life was of no significance. The only significant reality was *eternity*, on whose advent through death the "busy" monks were unwaveringly focused.

9 Simone de Beauvoir, *The Ethics of Ambiguity*, p. 122. Sartre's idea of "detotalized totalities" can be found in *The Philosophy of Jean-Paul Sartre*, edited by R. D. Cumming, in the chapter entitled "Consciousness and Society," pp. 415-84.

10 De Beauvoir, *Ethics of Ambiguity*, pp. 135-36.

11 Ibid., p. 125.

12 For Sartre's analysis of the possibility of "bad faith" in a consciousness reflective on itself, see *Being and Nothingness*, pp. 86-116.

13 Mary Renault, *The Last of the Wine*, reminiscent of the notion of friendship in Plato's *Symposium*, is one of Renault's beautiful and scholarly novels on life in ancient Greece.

14 De Beauvoir, *Ethics of Ambiguity*, p. 127.

15 Ibid., p. 128.

16 Hartshorne, Review of *Science and the Idea of God* by William E. Hocking, *Philosophy of Phenomenological Research* 6:454, 1945-1946.

17 De Beauvoir, *Ethics of Ambiguity*, p. 131.

18 Ibid.

19 This idea of being beyond any limit that one explicitly recognizes was the insight Socrates had when he realized that he was indeed the wisest of the Athenians, as the Delphic oracle had said, because "he knew that he did not know." We find essentially the same point in Hegel, when he criticizes Kant for rendering reason finite, since reason was clearly aware of its own finitude. See G. W. F. Hegel, *Encyclopaedia of the Philosophical Sciences*, Part I, *The Science of Logic*, pp. 82-120. In Bergson's *Two Sources of*

Morality and Religion we see how man devises all sorts of resistances against the horror of death which his intellectual consciousness makes present to him. One of these resistances is the notion of "immortality" (pp. 129-38). Ludwig Wittgenstein also has an intriguing remark on this matter in the realm of expression and language, for which see *Tractatus Logico-Philosophicus*, p. 3.

20 Elisabeth Kübler-Ross, *On Death and Dying*. This is a truly unique experiment. David Dempsey, in "Learning How To Die," gives an updated version of Kübler-Ross' seminars in the November 14, 1971 issue of *The New Times Magazine* (121:58-60, 64-74, 81). See also Milton M. Gatch, *Death: Meaning and Mortality in Christian Thought and Contemporary Culture*, for some contemporary Christian writing on death and immortality. And in *Death in Venice*, Thomas Mann portrays Plato's *eros* as an intense desire which consumes an artist as he dies watching the beauty of a young boy standing amidst a kaleidoscopic sea.

21 Henri Bergson writes: "Man is the only animal whose actions are uncertain, who hesitates, gropes about and lays plans in the hope of success and the fear of failure. He is alone in realizing that he is subject to illness, alone in knowing he must die" (*Two Sources of Morality and Religion*, p. 204). "Cases of animal suicide have been reported, but there is a vast difference between doing what must result in death, and knowing that the result will be death; to perform an action, even one that is well-contrived and appropriate is one thing; to forecast the outcome of it is another" (Ibid., p. 130).

22 Aquinas, *Quodlibetales*, 1, a. 8. This is a key article in Aquinas on the question of selfish and unselfish love of God in a creature, and contains his part-whole solution.

23 Marcel, *Mystery of Being*, vol. 2, p. 171. On this point Miguel de Unamuno y Jugo writes: "Man is perishable. That may be; but let us perish resisting, and if it is nothingness that awaits us, do not let us so act that it shall be a just fate" (*Tragic Sense of Life*, p. 260). Another writer puts it this way: "Certainly to know that a moral order belongs to the very nature of things, and is no mere figment of man's imagination, is not to know everything we should like to know about this universe. . . . But it is to know (or so it seems to me) that which effectively eliminates the most haunting of those ultimate fears that chill the heart of reflective man, the fear that human existence has no meaning or purpose beyond itself. For it is just not possible to believe that the moral order is objectively real—that there really are obligations unconditionally binding upon us as human beings to behave in certain ways—and to believe also that human existence has no meaning and purpose beyond itself" (Campbell, *On Selfhood and Godhood*, p. 206).

C. S. Lewis in one place makes an interesting point that may perhaps prove too much. He argues that a master's personality is so truly internalized in his pet, v. g., a dog, that such an animal, as differeniated from his wild counterpart in the jungle who never shared human influence, shares the human destiny of survival after death. "And in this way it seems to me possible that certain animals may have an immortality, not in themselves, but in the immortality of their masters. If you ask where its personal identity resides, I answer 'where its identity always did reside even in earthly life—in its relation to the Body, and especially to the master who is the head of that Body'" (*The Problem of Pain*, pp. 139-40). In another direction, that of literary imagination, we find Eugene O'Neill making the same point in an artistic way. He wrote a "last will and testament" for his Dalmatian dog, Blemie, to comfort his wife Carlotta before the dog died of old age in December 1940. In the document, O'Neill imagines Blemie saying: "Dogs do not fear death as men do. We accept it as part of life, not as something alien and terrible which destroys life. What may come after death, who knows? I would like to believe with those of my fellow dalmatians, who are devout Mohammedans, that there is a Paradise where one is always young and full-bladdered; where all the day one dillies and dallies with an amorous multitude of houris, beautifully spotted; where jackrabbits that run fast but not too fast (like the houris) are as the sands of the desert; where each blissful hour is mealtime; where in long evenings there are a million fireplaces with logs forever burning, and one curls up and blinks into the flames and nods and dreams, remembering the old brave days on earth, and the love of one's Master and Mistress" ("Last Will and Testament of Silver Dene Emblem O'Neill," *Look* 35:40, April 20, 1971).

BIBLIOGRAPHY

The following list includes those works which are cited explicitly in the text. In addition, there are a dozen or so other works which, although not cited, were formative influences in composing this book.

BOOKS

Adler, Mortimer J. *The Conditions of Philosophy: Its Checkered Past, Its Present Disorder, and Its Future Promise.* New York: Atheneum Publishers, 1965.
———— *The Idea of Freedom.* 2 vols. New York: Doubleday and Company, 1958, 1961.

Aquinas, St. Thomas. *Treatise on Man.* Translated by James F. Anderson. Englewood Cliffs, New Jersey: Prentice-Hall, 1962.

Ardrey, Robert. *African Genesis.* New York: Dell Publishing Company, 1961.

Bakan, David. *The Duality of Human Existence.* Chicago: Rand McNally and Company, 1966.

Báñez, Domingo. *The Primacy of Existence in Thomas Aquinas: A Commentary in Thomistic Metaphysics.* Translated with introduction and notes by Benjamin S. Llamzon. Chicago: Henry Regnery Company, 1966.
———— *Scholastica Commentaria in Primam Partem S. T.* Reprinted Edition. Dubuque, Iowa: William C. Brown Company, n.d.

Barnard, Christiaan Neethling, and C. B. Pepper. *Christiaan Barnard: One Life.* New York: The Macmillan Company, 1969.

Beauvoir, Simone de. *The Ethics of Ambiguity.* Translated by B. Frechtman. New York: Citadel Press, 1968.

Berdiaev, Nicolai. *Solitude and Society*. Translated by George Reavey. London: Centenary, 1938.

Berdyaev, Nicolas. *The Destiny of Man*. New York: Harper and Row, Publishers, 1960.

Berger, Peter L. *A Rumor of Angels*. New York: Doubleday and Company, 1969.

Bergson, Henri. *Time and Free Will*. Translated by F. L. Pogson. New York: Harper and Brothers, 1960.

———— *The Two Sources of Morality and Religion*. Translated by R. Ashley Audra and Cloudesley Brereton, with assistance of W. Horsfall Carter. New York: Doubleday, Doran and Company, 1935.

Bertocci, Peter. *Sex, Love, and the Person*. New York: Sheed and Ward, 1967.

Binswanger, Ludwig. *Sigmund Freud: Reminiscences of a Friendship*. Translated by Norbert Guterman. New York: Grune and Stratton, 1957.

Bonhoeffer, Dietrich. *Creation and Fall: Temptation*. Translated by J. C. Fletcher. New York: The Macmillan Company, 1959.

———— *Ethics*. Edited by E. Bethge. Translated by Neville Horton Smith. New York: The Macmillan Company, 1955.

———— *Letters and Papers from Prison*. Edited by Eberhard Bethge. Translated by R. Fuller and revised by F. Clarke and others. London: S.C.M. Press, 1953, 1967.

Bourke, Vernon J. *Will in Western Thought*. New York: Sheed and Ward, 1964.

Bradley, Francis H. *Ethical Studies*. Indianapolis: Bobbs-Merrill Company, 1951.

Brontë, Emily. *Wuthering Heights*. New York: Washington Square Press, 1960.

Brown, Norman O. *Life Against Death*. New York: Vintage Books, 1959.

———— *Love's Body*. New York: Vintage Books, 1966.

Buber, Martin. *Tales of the Hasidim*. Translated by Olga Marx. 2 vols. New York: Schocken Books, 1947, 1948.

Campbell, C. A. *On Selfhood and Godhood*. New York: The Macmillan Company, 1957.

Camus, Albert. *The Myth of Sisyphus*. Translated by Justin O'Brien. New York: Vintage Books, 1955.

———— *The Plague*. Translated by S. Gilbert. New York: Alfred A. Knopf, 1948.

Cervantes, Miguel de. *Don Quixote*. Translated by C. Jarvus. New York: The Pocket Library, 1957.

Clark, Kenneth. *Civilisation*. New York: Harper and Row, Publishers, 1969.

Cole, J. Preston. *The Problematic Self in Kierkegaard and Freud*. New Haven: Yale University Press, 1971.

Cornford, Francis M. *Plato's Theory of Knowledge*. New York: Liberal Arts Press, 1957.

Cory, Daniel. *Santayana: The Later Years*. New York: George Braziller, 1963.

Cumming, R. D., editor. *The Philosophy of Jean-Paul Sartre*. New York: Random House, 1965.

D'Arcy, Martin, S.J. *The Mind and Heart of Love*. New York: Meridian Books; Cleveland: The World Publishing Company, 1956.

Dewart, Leslie. *The Foundations of Belief*. New York: Herder and Herder, 1969.
—— *The Future of Belief*. New York: Herder and Herder, 1966.
—— *Religion, Language, and Truth*. New York: Herder and Herder, 1970.
Dewey, John. *Experience and Nature*. New York: Dover Publications, 1958.
—— *Theory of the Moral Life*. New York: Holt, Rinehart and Winston, 1960.
Donceel, J. F., S.J. *Philosophical Anthropology*. New York: Sheed and Ward, 1967.
Engel, S. Morris. *Language and Illumination*. The Hague: M. Nijhoff, 1969.
Erwin, Edward. *The Concept of Meaninglessness*. Baltimore: The Johns Hopkins Press, 1970.
Feifel, Herman, editor. *The Meaning of Death*. New York: McGraw-Hill Book Company, 1965.
Ferrater Mora, José. *Being and Death: An Outline of Integrationist Philosophy*. Berkeley and Los Angeles: University of California Press, 1965.
Fingarette, Herbert. *The Self in Transformation*. New York: Harper and Row, Publishers, 1963.
Frankl, Viktor E. *Man's Search for Meaning: An Introduction to Logotherapy*. New York: Washington Square Press, 1959.
Galilei, Galileo. *Discoveries and Opinions of Galileo*. Translated by S Drake. New York: Anchor Books, 1957.
Gallagher, Kenneth. *The Philosophy of Gabriel Marcel*. New York: Fordham University Press, 1962.
Gatch, Milton M. *Death: Meaning and Mortality in Christian Thought and Contemporary Culture*. New York: The Seabury Press, 1969.
Gilson, Etienne. *The Christian Philosophy of Saint Augustine*. Translated by L. E. M. Lynch. New York: Random House, 1960.
—— *The Christian Philosophy of St. Thomas Aquinas*. Translated by L. K. Shook, with "A Catalogue of St. Thomas's Works" by I. T. Eschmann, O.P. New York: Random House, 1956.
—— *The Mystical Theology of Saint Bernard*. Translated by A. H. C. Downes. New York: Sheed and Ward, 1940.
—— *The Spirit of Mediaeval Philosophy*. Translated by A. H. C. Downes. New York: Charles Scribner's Sons, 1936.
Goffman, Erving. *Behavior in Public Places*. New York: The Free Press of Glencoe, 1963.
Gould, Thomas. *Platonic Love*. New York: The Free Press of Glencoe, 1963.
Grunwald, H. A., editor. *Sex in America*. New York: Bantam Books, 1964.
Hallie, Philip P., editor. *Scepticism, Man and God: Selections from Major Writings of Sextus Empiricus*. Middletown, Connecticut: Wesleyan University Press, 1964.
Hazo, Robert G. *The Idea of Love*. The Institute of Philosophical Research. New York: Frederick A. Praeger, 1967.
Hegel, G. W. F. *Encyclopaedia of the Philosophical Sciences*. Part I, *The Science of Logic*. Translated by W. Wallace. Clarendon, England: Oxford University Press, 1892.

Hegel, G. W. F. *The Phenomenology of Mind*. Translated by J. B. Baillie. New York: Harper and Row, Publishers, 1967.

Homans, Peter. *Theology after Freud*. Indianapolis: Bobbs-Merrill Company, 1970.

Hopkins, Gerard M. *Poems*. New York: Oxford University Press, 1948.

Hume, David. *A Treatise of Human Nature*. New York: Doubleday and Company, 1961.

James, William. *Psychology*. Edited by G. W. Allport. New York: Harper and Row, Publishers, 1961.

———— *The Will To Believe*. New York: Dover Publications, 1956.

Janson, H. W., and D. J. Janson. *History of Art*. Englewood Cliffs, New Jersey: Prentice-Hall, 1969.

Johann, Robert O., S. J. *The Meaning of Love*. Glen Rock, New Jersey: Deus Books, 1966.

Johnstone, Henry W., Jr. *The Problem of the Self*. University Park: Pennsylvania State University, 1970.

Kant, Immanuel. *Critique of Judgment*. Translated by J. H. Bernard. New York: The Macmillan Company, 1931.

———— *Critique of Practical Reason*. Translated with introduction by Lewis W. Beck. Indianapolis: Bobbs-Merrill Company, 1956.

———— *Fundamental Principles of the Metaphysics of Morals*. Translated by Thomas K. Abbott, with introduction by Marvin Fox. Indianapolis: Bobbs-Merrill Company, 1949.

———— *On History*. Translated by L. W. Beck, R. E. Anchor, and E. L. Fackenheim. Indianapolis: Bobbs-Merrill Company, 1963.

Kelly, Amy R. *Eleanor of Aquitaine and the Four Kings*. Cambridge, Massachusetts: Harvard University Press, 1950.

Kierkegaard, Søren. *Concluding Unscientific Postscript*. Translated by D. F. Swenson and W. Lowrie. Princeton, New Jersey: Princeton University Press, 1941.

———— *Either/Or*. 2 vols. Vol I, translated by D. F. and L. M. Swenson; Vol. II, translated by W. Lowrie. Princeton, New Jersey: Princeton University Press, 1944.

———— *Fear and Trembling* and *The Sickness unto Death*. 2 vols. in 1. Translated by W. Lowrie. New York: Doubleday and Company, 1954.

———— *Philosophical Fragments*. Translated by D. F. Swenson. Princeton, New Jersey: Princeton University Press, 1936.

———— *The Sickness unto Death* and *Fear and Trembling*. 2 vols. in 1. Translated by W. Lowrie. New York: Doubleday and Company, 1954.

———— *Works of Love*. Translated by D. F. and L. Swenson. Princeton, New Jersey: Princeton University Press, 1946.

Klubertanz, George, S. J. *Habits and Virtues*. New York: Appleton-Century-Crofts, 1965.

Kolbe, F. C. *A Catholic View of Holism*. New York: The Macmillan Company, 1928.

Kübler-Ross, Elisabeth. *On Death and Dying*. New York: The Macmillan Company, 1969.

Leibniz, Gottfried W. *New Essays Concerning the Human Understanding*. Translated by A. G. Langley. New York: The Macmillan Company, 1896.

Levinas, Emmanuel. *Totality and Infinity*. Translated by A. Lingis. The Hague: M. Nijhoff, 1969.

Lewis, C. S. *The Allegory of Love*. New York: Oxford University Press, 1958.

———— *The Four Loves*. New York: Harcourt, Brace and Company, 1960.

———— *A Grief Observed*. Greenwich, Connecticut: The Seabury Press, 1961.

———— *The Problem of Pain*. New York: The Macmillan Company, 1962.

Lorenz, Konrad. *On Aggression*. Translated by Marjorie Kerr Wilson. New York: Bantam Books, 1966.

Lowrie, Walter. *Kierkegaard*. New York: Oxford University Press, 1938.

Mann, Thomas. *Death in Venice*. Translated by Kenneth Burke. New York: Bantam Books, 1925.

Marcel, Gabriel. *Being and Having: An Existentialist Diary*. Translated by K. Farrer. New York: Harper and Row, Publishers, 1965.

———— *Creative Fidelity*. Translated by R. Rosthal. New York: The Noonday Press, 1964.

———— *Homo Viator*. Translated by E. Craufurd. New York: Harper and Row, Publishers, 1962.

———— *The Mystery of Being*. 2 vols. Vol. 1, translated by G. S. Fraser; Vol. 2, translated by R. Hague. Chicago: Henry Regnery Company, 1960.

———— *Philosophy of Existence*. Translated by M. Harari. London: Harvill Press, 1948.

———— *Presence and Immortality*. Translated by M. A. Machado and revised by H. J. Koren. Pittsburgh: Duquesne University Press, 1967.

Marcuse, Herbert. *Eros and Civilization*. New York: Vintage Books, 1962.

———— *One Dimensional Man*. Boston: Beacon Press, 1966.

Maslow, Abraham. *Toward a Psychology of Being*. New York: Van Nostrand-Reinhold Company, 1968.

May, Rollo. *Love and Will*. New York: W. W. Norton and Company, 1969.

Mayeroff, Milton. *On Caring*. New York: Harper and Row, Publishers, 1971.

Merleau-Ponty, Maurice. *Phenomenology of Perception*. Translated by C. Smith. New York: Humanities Press, 1962.

Montagu, Ashley, editor. *Man and Aggression*. New York: Oxford University Press, 1968.

Morgan, Douglas N. *Love: Plato, the Bible and Freud*. Englewood Cliffs, New Jersey: Prentice-Hall, 1964.

Morris, Desmond. *The Human Zoo*. New York: McGraw-Hill Book Company, 1969.

Munson, Thomas, S. J. *The Essential Wisdom of George Santayana*. New York: Columbia University Press, 1962.

Munz, P. *Relationship and Solitude*. London: Eyre and Spottiswoode, 1964.

Murray, John Courtney, S. J. *We Hold These Truths*. New York: Sheed and Ward, 1960.

Myers, Gerald E. *Self*. New York: Pegasus, 1969.

Natanson, Maurice. *The Journeying Self: A Study in Philosophy and Social Role*. Reading, Massachusetts: Addison-Wesley Publishing Company, 1970.

Nédoncelle, Maurice. *God's Encounter with Man: A Contemporary Approach to Prayer.* Translated by A. Manson. New York: Sheed and Ward, 1964.
―――― *Love and the Person.* Translated by R. Adelaide. New York: Sheed and Ward, 1966.
Nietzsche, Friedrich. *Thus Spake Zarathustra.* In *Portable Nietzsche,* edited by W. Kaufmann. New York: The Viking Press, 1954.
Nygren, Anders. *Agape and Eros.* Translated by P. S. Watson. Philadelphia: The Westminster Press, 1953.
O'Brien, Denis. *Empedocles' Cosmic Cycle.* London: Cambridge University Press, 1969.
O'Brien, Michael J. *The Socratic Paradoxes and the Greek Mind.* Chapel Hill: University of North Carolina Press, 1967.
Organ, Troy W. *The Self in Indian Philosophy.* The Hague: Mouton and Company, 1964.
Pegis, A. C. *At the Origins of the Thomistic Notion of Man.* New York: The Macmillan Company, 1963.
Pernoud, Régine. *Eleanor of Aquitaine.* Translated by P. Wiles. New York: Coward-McCann, 1968.
Polanyi, Michael. *The Tacit Dimension.* New York: Doubleday and Company, 1966.
Portalié, Eugène, S.J. *A Guide to the Thought of Saint Augustine.* Translated by Ralph J. Bastian, S.J. Chicago: Henry Regnery Company, 1960.
Rand, Ayn. *The Virtue of Selfishness.* New York: Signet Book, 1964.
Renault, Mary. *The Last of the Wine.* New York: Pantheon Books, 1956.
Richardson, Herbert W. *Nun, Witch, Playmate.* New York: Harper and Row, Publishers, 1971.
Ricoeur, Paul. *Fallible Man.* Translated by C. Kelbley. Chicago: Henry Regnery Company, 1965.
―――― *Freud and Philosophy: An Essay on Interpretation.* Translated by D. Savage. New Haven: Yale University Press, 1970.
Rieff, Philip. *Freud: The Mind of the Moralist.* New York: The Viking Press, 1959.
―――― *The Triumph of the Therapeutic.* New York: Harper and Row, Publishers, 1968.
Robinson, John A. T. *Christian Morals Today.* Philadelphia: The Westminster Press, 1964.
―――― *Honest to God.* Philadelphia: The Westminster Press, 1963.
Ross, Sir David. *Plato's Theory of Ideas.* New York: Oxford University Press, 1951.
Rougemont, Denis de. *Passion and Society.* Translated by M. Belgion. London: Faber and Faber, 1956.
Rousselot, Pierre. *Pour L'Histoire du Problème de L'Amour Au Moyen Age.* Munster: Aschendorffschen Buchhandlung, 1908.
Sadler, William A. *Existence and Love.* New York: Charles Scribner's Sons, 1969.

Santayana, George. *Persons and Places.* Vol. 1, *The Background of My Life.* New York: Charles Scribner's Sons, 1944.

Sartre, Jean-Paul. *Being and Nothingness.* Translated by H. E. Barnes. New York: Washington Square Press, 1953.

Scheler, Max. *The Nature of Sympathy.* Translated by B. Noble. New York: Harper and Brothers, 1960.

Schopenhauer, Arthur. *The World as Will and Idea.* Translated by R. B. Haldane and J. Kemp. Vol. 3. London: Routledge and Kegan Paul, 1948.

Schur, Max. *Freud: Living and Dying.* New York: International Universities Press, 1972.

Shideler, Mary M. *The Theology of Romantic Love: A Study in the Writings of Charles Williams.* New York: Harper and Row, Publishers, 1962.

Skinner, B. F. *Beyond Freedom and Dignity.* New York: Alfred A. Knopf, 1971.

Slaatte, Howard A. *The Pertinence of the Paradox.* New York: Humanities Press, 1968.

Teilhard de Chardin, Pierre. *The Divine Milieu.* Translated by B. Wall. New York: Harper and Brothers, 1960.

————— *The Phenomenon of Man.* Translated by B. Wall. New York: Harper and Brothers, 1959.

Tennyson, Alfred Lord. *Complete Poetical Works.* Boston: Houghton Mifflin Company, 1898.

Thomte, Reidar. *Kierkegaard's Philosophy of Religion.* Princeton, New Jersey: Princeton University Press, 1948.

Thoreau, Henry D. *Walden.* New York: Doubleday and Company, 1960.

Tolstoy, Leo. *Anna Karenina.* New York: Penguin Books, 1954.

Toner, Jules, S. J. *The Experience of Love.* Washington, D. C.: Corpus Instrumentorum, 1968.

Unamuno y Jugo, Miguel de. *Tragic Sense of Life.* Translated by J. E. C. Flitch. New York: Dover Publications, 1954.

Vander Veer, Garrett L. *Bradley's Metaphysics and the Self.* New Haven: Yale University Press, 1970.

Vonnegut, Kurt. *Cat's Cradle.* New York: Holt, Rinehart and Winston, 1963.

————— *Mother Night.* New York: Harper and Row, Publishers, 1966.

Walker, Curtis H. *Eleanor of Aquitaine.* Chapel Hill: University of North Carolina Press, 1950.

Whitehead, Alfred N. *Religion in the Making.* New York: Meridian Books, 1960.

————— *Science and the Modern World.* New York: The Free Press, 1967.

Wicks, Jared. *Man Yearning for Grace.* Washington, D. C.: Corpus Instrumentorum, 1968.

Wilder, Thornton. *Three Plays.* New York: Harper and Brothers, 1957.

Wittgenstein, Ludwig. *Philosophical Investigations.* Translated by G. E. M. Anscombe. New York: The Macmillan Company, 1953.

————— *Tractatus Logico-Philosophicus.* Translated by D. F. Pears and B. F. McGuinness. London: Routledge and Kegan Paul, 1961.

ARTICLES AND ESSAYS

Allison, H. E. "Faith and Falsifiability." *The Review of Metaphysics* 22:508-22, March 1969.

Armstrong, A. H. "Platonic Eros and Christian Agape." *Downside Review* 79:105-21, September 1961.

Barrose, T. "The Unity of the Two Charities in Greek Patristic Exegesis." *Theological Studies* 15:355-88, September 1954.

Becker, Ernest. "The Evaded Question: Science and Human Nature." *Commonweal* 89:638-50, February 21, 1969.

Calderone, Mary. "The Case for Chastity." In *Sex in America*, edited by H. A. Grunwald, pp. 140-41. New York: Bantam Books, 1964.

Cantin, S. "Henri Bergson et le Probleme de la Liberté." *Laval Theologique et Philosophique* 1:71-102, 1945.

Cronan, E. P., S.S. "Bergson and Free Will." *The New Scholasticism* 11:1-57, January 1937.

Dempsey, David. "Learning How To Die." *The New York Times Magazine* 121:58-60, 64-74, 81, November 14, 1971.

Doherty, Dennis. "Consummation and the Indissolubility of Marriage." In *Absolutes in Moral Theology?* edited by Charles Curran, pp. 211-31. Washington, D. C.: Corpus Instrumentorum, 1968.

Dupré, Louis. "The Constitution of the Self in Kierkegaard's Philosophy." *International Philosophical Quarterly* 3:506-26, December 1963.

Eames, S. Morris. "Dewey's Theory of Valuation." In *Guide to the Works of John Dewey*, edited by Jo Ann Boydston, pp. 183-99. Carbondale: Southern Illinois University Press, 1970.

Eslick, Leonard. "The Dyadic Character of Being in Plato." *The Modern Schoolman* 21:11-18, November 1953.

——— "Plato on Being." *The Modern Schoolman* 36:205-08, March 1959.

——— "Plato's Dialectic on Non-Being." *The New Scholasticism* 29:33-39, January 1955.

——— "The Real Distinction between Essence and Existence." *The Modern Schoolman* 38:149-60, January 1961.

Fisher, John H. "Tristan and Courtly Adultery." *Comparative Literature* 9:150-64, Spring 1967.

Gregory, T. S. Review of *Agape and Eros. Month* 11:221-34, April 1954.

Hartshorne, Charles. Review of *Science and the Idea of God* by William E. Hocking. *Philosophy of Phenomenological Research* 6:453-56, 1945-1946.

Holloway, Maurice R., S.J. "Towards the Fullness of Being." In *Proceedings, Jesuit Philosophical Association*, pp. 1-23. Woodstock, Maryland, 1962.

Hook, Sidney. "The Desirable and Emotive in Dewey's Ethics." In *John Dewey, Philosopher of Science and Freedom*, edited by S. Hook, pp. 194-216. New York: Barnes and Noble, 1950.

Hughes, Herman, S.J. "This Mediaeval Winter." *America* 120:156-58, February 8, 1969.

Koninck, Charles de. "General Standards and Particular Situations in Relation to Natural Law." In *Proceedings, American Catholic Philosophical Association*, Vol. 24, pp. 28-32. Washington, D. C., 1950.

Lifton, Robert J. "The Young and the Old." *The Atlantic Monthly* 224:47-54, September 1969.

Llamzon, Benjamin S. "The Specification of Esse." *The Modern Schoolman* 41:123-43, January 1964.

———— "Supposital and Accidental Esse." *The New Scholasticism* 39:170-88, April 1965.

Lynch, William F. "Psychological Man." *America* 117:635-37, November 25, 1967.

Marcuse, Herbert. "Repressive Tolerance." In *A Critique of Pure Tolerance*, by K. Wolff, B. Moore, and H. Marcuse, pp. 81-123. Boston: Beacon Press, 1969.

Martin, Anne. "Time To Grow in Love." In *What Modern Catholics Think about Birth Control*, edited by W. Birmingham, pp. 191-204. New York: Signet Book, 1964.

Murchland, Bernard. "Between Solitude and Solidarity." *Commonweal* 93:91-95, October 23, 1970.

O'Neill, Eugene. "Last Will and Testament of Silver Dene Emblem O'Neill." *Look* 35:39-40, April 20, 1971.

Pax, Clyde. "Philosophical Reflection: Gabriel Marcel." *The New Scholasticism* 38:159-77, April 1964.

Roazen, Paul. "A Curious Triangle: Freud, Lou Andreas-Salomé and Victor Tausk." *Encounter* 33:83-89, October 1969.

Russell, Jeffrey B. "Courtly Love as Religious Dissent." *Catholic Historical Review* 51:31-44, April 1965.

Schaldenbrand, Mary. "Freedom and the I: An Existential Inquiry." *International Philosophical Quarterly* 3:571-99, December 1963.

———— "Gabriel Marcel: Philosopher of Intersubjectivity." In *Twentieth-Century Thinkers*, edited by J. K. Ryan, pp. 107-30. Staten Island: Alba House, 1965.

———— "Self-Becoming and the Other." *Thought* 41:413-37, Autumn 1966.

———— "Time, the Self and Hope." In *The Future as the Presence of Shared Hope*, edited by M. Muckenhirn, pp. 112-29. New York: Sheed and Ward, 1968.

Schmemann, Alexander. "The Indissolubility of Marriage: The Theological Tradition of the East." In *The Bond of Marriage*, edited by W. W. Bassett, pp. 97-116. Notre Dame, Indiana: University of Notre Dame Press, 1968.

Schneider, Herbert W., and Darnell Rucker. "Dewey's Ethics." In *Guide to the Works of John Dewey*, edited by Jo Ann Boydston, pp. 99-130. Carbondale: Southern Illinois University Press, 1970.

Siewert, Donald J. "The Body in Marcel's Metaphysics." *Thought* 46:389-405, Autumn 1971.

Stanmeyer, William. "The Jurisprudence of Radical Change: Herbert Marcuse's 'Great Refusal' Vs. Political Due Process." *St. John's Law Review* 45:1-38, October 1970.

Vlastos, Gregory. "The Unity of the Virtues in the *Protagoras*." *The Review of Metaphysics* 25:415-58, March 1972.

SOURCES

Aquinas, St. Thomas. *Basic Writings.* Edited by A. C. Pegis. 2 vols. New York: Random House, 1945.

──── *Opera Omnia.* Vols. I, II, III, V, VI, VIII, IX. Parma, 1852-1873.

Aristotle. *Basic Works.* Edited by Richard McKeon. New York: Random House, 1941.

Augustine, St. *Basic Writings.* Edited by W. J. Oates. 2 vols. New York: Random House, 1948.

──── *Corpus Christianorum: Series Latina.* Vols. 32, 40, 48, 50. Turnholti: Typographi Brepols Editores Pontifici, 1955-1969.

Descartes, René. *Philosophical Works.* Translated by E. S. Haldane and G. Ross. 2 vols. New York: Dover Publications, 1955.

──── *Vie et Oeuvres.* Vol. 12, by C. Adam. Paris: Cerf, 1910.

Duns Scotus, Joannes. *Commentaria Oxoniensia ad IV Libros Magistri Sententiarum.* Edited by M. F. Garcia. 2 vols. Quaracchi, 1912.

Freud, Sigmund. *Collected Papers.* Translated under supervision of Joan Riviere. 5 vols. New York: Basic Books, 1959.

──── *Gesammelte Werke.* Vols. 13, 14, 16. London: Imago Publishing Company, 1953.

──── *Standard Edition.* Translated under editorship of James Strachey. Vols. 11, 13, 14, 18, 19, 21, 23. London: Hogarth Press, 1955─.

Jones, Ernest. *The Life and Work of Sigmund Freud.* 3 vols. New York: Basic Books, 1953-1957.

Luther, Martin. *Works.* Vol. 34, edited by Lewis W. Spitz; Vol. 44, edited by James Atkinson. St. Louis: Concordia Publishing House, 1960, 1966.

Migne, J.-P. *Patrologia Latina.* Vols. 34, 37, 38, 41, 42, 44. Paris: 1854─.

Mill, John S. *Collected Works.* Edited by J. M. Robson. Vol. 10. Toronto: University of Toronto Press, 1969.

Plato. *The Dialogues.* Translated by B. Jowett. 2 vols. New York: Random House, 1937.

Tolstoy, Leo N. *Novels and Other Works.* Edited by Nathan Dole. Vol. 17. New York: Charles Scribner's Sons, 1902.

ACKNOWLEDGMENTS

I thank all the publishers whose books I quoted. I am especially grateful for specific permission to publish quotes:

Excerpted from pp. 412, 453, Volume 2 and p. 340, Volume 3, in *The Collected Papers of Sigmund Freud*, by Ernest Jones, Basic Books, Inc., Publishers, New York, 1959.

From Herbert Marcuse: *Eros and Civilization*, Beacon Press, Boston.

From Immanuel Kant: *Fundamental Principles of the Metaphysics of Morals*, translated by Thomas K. Abbott, copyright, 1949, by The Liberal Arts Press, Inc., reprinted by permission of The Bobbs-Merrill Company, Inc.

From Simone de Beauvoir: *The Ethics of Ambiguity*, translated by B. Frechtman, Citadel Press, New York.

From William James: *The Will To Believe*; and John Dewey: *Experience and Nature*, Dover Publications, Inc., New York.

From Gabriel Marcel: *Presence and Immortality*, translated by M. A. Machado and revised by H. J. Koren; and Emmanuel Levinas: *Totality and Infinity*, translated by A. Lingis, Duquesne University Press, Pittsburgh.

From Gabriel Marcel: *Creative Fidelity*, translated by R. Rosthal, © 1964, Noonday Press, Farrar, Straus & Giroux, Inc., New York.

From Kenneth Gallagher: *The Philosophy of Gabriel Marcel*, Fordham University Press, New York.

From Gabriel Marcel: *Being and Having*, translated by K. Farrer; Nicolas Berdyaev: *The Destiny of Man*; and Philip Rieff: *The Triumph of the Therapeutic*, Harper and Row, Publishers, Inc., New York.

From Gabriel Marcel: *Homo Viator*, translated by E. Craufurd; *The Mystery of Being*, translated by G. S. Fraser; and Paul Ricoeur: *Fallible Man*, translated by C. Kelbley, Henry Regnery Company, Chicago.

INDEX

About this book

The Self Beyond was set in the composing room of Loyola University Press. The text is 11 on 14 Caledonia; the reduced matter is 9 on 12; and the notes 8 on 10. The display type is 12 Caledonia.

It was printed and bound by R. R. Donnelley & Sons Company, using the Cameron Book System on International's Dontext 55-pound offwhite paper and bound in Holliston Sturdite No. 24.

"The tang of living comes, to a great extent," says the author of this book, "in baring one's self to others." For that is at the heart of the "wholing" process he sees as an answer to the "meaning of life" question which has troubled philosophers through the ages and tugs at the edges of every man's mind. Can a man find a meaning to life that carries even beyond the grave, and how can a man build meaningful bridges between himself and those he loves, beyond his own self to those about him, beyond time to eternity?

The author's answer, expressed in the concept of "wholing" one's life, of achieving self-fulfillment, and then reaching out to ever wider "wholes," is a joyous and optimistic philosophy, a far cry from the sad, sometimes lonely and even despairing answers of those who today would ask if life is worth living. Yes, this is a book of philosophical exploration, but not of the sterile, technical classroom variety. For it contains passages of inspiring beauty and practical consequence for the reader who wonders what he should make—indeed, what he can make—of his life.

Benjamin S. Llamzon was born and educated in the Philippines. In 1957, he came to the United States to do doctoral studies at St. Louis University. But that was only